LIVING WORDS IN EPHESIANS

Wayne Detzler

 EVANGELICAL PRESS

EVANGELICAL PRESS
16/18 High Street, Welwyn, Hertfordshire
AL6 9EQ, England.

First published 1981

ISBN 0 85234-157-1

Bible quotations are from the New International Version

Typeset in Great Britain by 'Altair', 86 Tilehouse Street, Hitchin, Herts.
Printed in USA.

*To the members and friends of
Kensington Baptist Church, Bristol,
for their loving, prayerful support.*

Contents

Preface

The communication and application of the Scriptures are my main aim. Too often the treasures of the Greek text are locked away in the safe vaults of academic literature and lectures. These word studies arise out of the expository preaching of Ephesians during the winter of 1979-80 at Kensington Baptist Church in Bristol.

Two main tools have assisted me in preparing these studies. The basic Greek lexicon is William F. Arndt and F. Wilbur Gingrich, *Greek-English Lexicon of the New Testament*, 2nd edition (Chicago: University of Chicago Press, 1979). Further invaluable aid has been derived from Robert Young, *Analytical Concordance to the Bible* (Grand Rapids: Wm. B. Eerdmans Publishing Company, 1955).

It is my prayer that these short studies will be practically helpful to Sunday School teachers, lay preachers and serious students of the Scriptures. I also acknowledge my debt of gratitude to Mrs V. Williams and Mrs Marjorie Mowbray for their assistance in typing and editing the text.

Wayne A. Detzler
Bristol, February 1981

1.
Saints alive

Paul pens Ephesians with specific people in mind: 'the saints in Ephesus' (Ephesians 1:1). The word translated 'saints' comes from a very illustrious family. The Old Testament Hebrew word is *kadosh*. In the New Testament the Greek equivalent is *hagios*. English translations include such terms as 'holy', 'sanctified' and 'saints'. Saints are by definition those whom God has set apart and made holy.

From the beginning of biblical revelation, God planned to produce a race of saints. As far back as the book of Exodus, He expressed this purpose for His stubborn and often rebellious people, the Jews. Through Moses, Jehovah told the Jews, 'You will be for me a kingdom of priests and a holy nation' (Exodus 19:6).

His instruction to Israel is unmistakable: 'I am the Lord your God; consecrate yourselves and be holy, because I am holy ... Be holy' (Leviticus 11:44-45). This decree is repeated in the New Testament, but by this time it refers to the saints. According to Peter, they are called by God to be a 'chosen people, a royal priesthood, a holy nation, a people belonging to God, that you may declare the praises of Him who called you out of darkness into His wonderful light' (1 Peter 2:9). Like Israel, the New Testament chosen ones are commanded: 'Be holy, because I am holy' (1 Peter 1:16).

Just as a parent often says, 'Act your age', so God expects us to act as saints. By grace He saves us and gives us the Holy Spirit to enable us to be holy; then He instructs us to act in a holy way. Needless to say, holiness does not characterize every believer. In fact, no believer acts up to this divine standard.

Still God calls them 'saints'. At salvation God places us in the position of saints. Already this spiritual potential is present in each of us. During our lifetime God the Holy Spirit is busy trimming off the unholy edges of our lives.

How do these saints look in the flesh? This can best be determined by observing what they are *not*. Saints are not sinlessly perfect. Writing to the quarrelsome congregation at Corinth, Paul introduced his first letter by calling them 'the church of God at Corinth, those sanctified in Christ Jesus and called to be holy' (1 Corinthians 1:2). Subsequent information reveals these saints to be schismatic, sexually perverse and sacrilegious. Perfect they were not.

Saints are also not necessarily spiritually mature. Although some have regarded the Philippian church as a collection of the completely sanctified, a hard look at Philippians disproves this. They were disunited and Paul warned them to be 'like-minded, having the same love, being one in spirit and purpose' (Philippians 2:2). The cause of this was probably selfishness, for he exhorts them to 'do nothing out of selfish ambition or vain conceit' (Philippians 2:3).

New Testament saints were also not self-made men. The Roman Christians had never enjoyed an apostolic visit. Their church was not the result of any human effort, but their spiritual position rested wholly on the call and love of God (Romans 1:7). Paul reminded them that their sainthood was based on grace alone.

The Ephesian Christians benefited by the longest stop in Paul's ministry, three years. They had a primary position among the churches in the Roman province of Asia. Timothy, that selfless saint, served them as pastor. Nevertheless, Paul reminded them that their completion in holiness was still a future event (Ephesians 1:4; 5:26).

Take comfort! The first-century Christians who basked in the light of immediate apostolic revelation were not completely sanctified, and neither are we. We are God's 'construction zone' and He is hard at work making us in practice what we are in potential — saints.

Saints are real people

Saints in biblical terms were not those who had arrived. The question is 'What did they look like while they were on the road?' The answer is that they were common people who performed uncommon exploits by God's grace and in His name. Both the Bible and subsequent history give us some credible examples.

In the Old Testament God chose very ordinary men to speak for Him. Amos was a shepherd from Tekoa, rustic in appearance and righteous in behaviour. God saw him as a powerful prophet capable of confronting an idolatrous people.

Hundreds of years later, the Lord called a collection of rather ordinary Jews to become disciples and apostles. One of the most unlikely was Simon Peter. His fishing business was not successful, in fact it was outstanding only when Jesus organized the catch. Peter's personality was vacillating at best. But God set him apart to be an apostle, and the crowd at Pentecost was moved to repentance.

Modern history abounds with similar stories. At the end of the eighteenth century, there was a common cobbler in England's Midlands. He fashioned a globe out of leather scraps and prayed for world missions. God touched Willam Carey, the humble shoemaker, and he became the father of the modern missionary movement.

A century later the same thing happened in America. A young lad was converted in Sunday School. His name was Dwight Lyman Moody. He, too, was in the shoe trade as a salesman. Then God set him apart, and he became the instrument through whom God brought revival to both Britain and the United States.

Perhaps an old illustration can further illuminate the word 'saints'. Saints are like a piece of coal dug out of a deep mine. Imagine the darkness, dampness and disease emanating from that subterranean source. No negative description can exaggerate 'the quarry from which [we] were hewn' (Isaiah 51:1).

A piece of coal is ultimately thrown into the fire together with other black chunks, some of which have been warmed already by the flame. Similarly, the saint is placed together with others who have been removed from the pit. In fact, the New Testament calls the church collectively 'called out ones' (*ekklesia*). The individual piece of coal soon starts to glow, ignited by its flaming neighbours. In the same way, Christians are warmed spiritually by the fellowship and teaching of the church. The Bible never speaks of saints in isolation, but always of 'saints' collectively. When a piece of coal is removed from the grate, it soon stops glowing. So it is with saints. They are lights in the world, but they constantly need to be warmed up in the fellowship of the church. It is a small wonder that the writer of Hebrews warned his readers: 'Let us not give up meeting together, as some are in the habit of doing, but let us encourage one another' (Hebrews 10:25).

Saints are not sickly sweet souls purporting to be 'holier than thou', but very common folks. The difference is not in them, but in their God.

2.
God's Choice

*'He **chose** us in him before the creation of the world'*
(Eph. 1:4)

The Scriptures seem to be much more concerned with the free will of God than with man's freedom of choice. At the outset God selected one man, Abraham, and made him the vehicle of divine revelation and redemption. From among Abraham's progeny God chose his grandson, Jacob. This choice baffled everybody, because the lad looked unqualified on both natural and moral grounds. Even Israel's greatest monarch, David, was chosen over his brothers who outstripped him in age and experience.

When we cross over into the New Testament, God's choosing is broadened to include a world-wide family of the faithful. The word used to connote God's choosing is *eklegomai*. There are at least three aspects of its meaning.

First, it entails the *selection* of someone or something *from among an array of alternatives*. The Lord told His disciples: 'I have chosen you out of the world' (John 15:19). Divine selection is seen dramatically in Acts 1, where two men are put forward as replacements for the suicidal traitor, Judas (v. 24). One, Matthias, is chosen apparently at random, but God governed the choice.

A second aspect of choosing is *personal possession*. A person chooses that which will give him pleasure and belong exclusively to him. In the great gospel treatise on election, the Lord asserts, 'You did not choose me, but I chose you to go and bear fruit' (John 15:16). It is very much like a made-to-measure suit. Its material is carefully selected along with the cut of the garment. The tailor employs his best skills to fit the trousers and jacket to the wearer's figure. Thus the end product is peculiarly 'suited' to its possessor. God made us for Himself, and we are thus chosen to be His.

The third concept implicit in the word is the *purpose* for which someone or something is chosen. In his devastatingly frank first letter to the Corinthians, the apostle Paul deflates the human ego with penetrating accuracy. God has chosen, according to Paul, the 'foolish', 'weak', 'lowly' and 'despised' to accomplish His plan (1 Corinthians 1:27-29). One thinks of the sculptor who resorts to the scrap yard and returns home with a car full of rusty, twisted metal. Only after cutting, welding, grinding and shaping does the finished image emerge. So God picks out the most unlikely pieces of human wreckage and shapes them into masterpieces of beauty. His purpose is evident to Him at the time of choosing. To us this purpose may only become visible later.

The elective activity of God embraces all three of the basic meanings in our Greek verb. In fact, selection, possession and purpose all characterize His dealings with His own men and women.

Don't twist the teaching!

Few biblical doctrines have been so misunderstood or assailed as this one. Breathe the word 'predestination' and normally placid people start to seethe. Obviously, part of this resistance may arise out of sheer stubborn opposition to biblical revelation. Most resist this teaching, however, because of an inadequate understanding of the total biblical context. There are at least four areas of misunderstanding.

First, *this doctrine does not mean that God is unjust.* 'How can a good God send people to hell?' is a frequent and emotive question. The real query is 'How can God choose some and not others?' These questions are only valid if some people really deserved to be saved. If there were a class of individuals or even just one who was good enough to please God, then He would be unjust in selecting some for salvation. Of course, none of us deserves God's grace. We have all fallen far short of His superhuman standard (Romans 3:23). Therefore, God's grace in choosing men and women for salvation is a thoroughly undeserved boon.

Second, *this doctrine does not rob man of his responsibility*. Man is not a robot programmed to please God, or a puppet dancing senselessly at the end of strings. God holds man responsible for his deeds. The complementary nature of human responsibility and divine sovereignty is seen in the New Testament. Looking forward to His crucifixion Jesus said, 'The Son of Man will go just as it is written about him. But woe to that man who betrays the Son of Man!' (Matthew 26:24.) God planned the sacrifice of the Saviour in the councils of eternity (Revelation 13:8), but the wicked men who did it were still held guilty at the bar of divine justice (Acts 2:23).

Third, *evangelism is not rendered invalid*. God commands believers to proclaim His good news to every human being (Mark 16:15). As we go to announce the gospel, we are confident that God is convicting men of sin (John 16:8-9), drawing people to Himself (John 6:44) and instilling faith in them. Does this sound illogical? It is also reflected in the world of agriculture. Every farmer knows that the success of his crop rests largely with 'nature', over which he has no control. Still he prepares the field, sows the best possible seed, cultivates and fertilizes in preparation and hope for the harvest. By the same token, God ordains that people will be saved; He also ordains that men are to bring salvation's story to their contemporaries. He plans both the end result and the means to reach it.

Fourth, *neither is this doctrine capable of logical explanation*. It is a paradox! In Romans 9:10-13 the illustration of Esau and Jacob is given. Why God chose the deceptive, slippery, thoroughly repulsive Jacob over his robust brother Esau is not clear to the Bible reader. The reason given by the apostle Paul is 'It does not, therefore, depend on man's desire or effort, but on God's mercy' (Romans 9:16). God will have the glory for Himself, and man has no claim to the credit. Someone said that human responsibility and divine sovereignty are like railway tracks which run parallel but appear to meet beyond the range of human vision. However, this illustration rests upon an optical illusion. These two great principles of biblical revelation are really reconciled in the infinite understanding of our loving God.

My reaction to this difficult doctrine must be belief. Although I cannot decipher it, I can accept it, just as I cannot comprehend how a brown cow eats green grass and yields white milk which turns into yellow butter, nevertheless I enjoy its products. Now we understand only part of God's revelation, but ultimately we 'shall know fully, even as [we are] fully known' (1 Corinthians 13:12).

3.
Mystery revealed

*'He made known to us the **mystery** of his will'* (Eph. 1:9)

'Mystery' conjures up in modern minds images of Sherlock Holmes and Agatha Christie. It is a dark plot to be untangled by assiduous and exhaustive detection methods. However, the New Testament writers understood something quite different when they wrote 'mystery', a word taken directly from the Greek *musterion*.

It carried stong overtones of the contemporary mystery religions. These ancient cults claimed possession of life-giving, secret knowledge. Only when one had undergone an elaborate initiation ritual and been admitted to the secret society could one know these mysteries. Under divine inspiration the apostle takes to hand this word as a weapon against its own exponents. The real mystery was not devised by ancient seers and passed down by successive wise men. Biblical mystery was born in the eternal mind of God. So perfect was this message that it could never have been constructed by man's puny wit. In Christ these mysteries were communicated to us.

The Lord referred to His kingdom teaching as 'mysteries' (Matthew 13:11, Greek). It was revealed to His disciples, although the stubborn Pharisees would not comprehend it. The kingdom was pictured in political hues by the Pharisees, but through parabolic teaching the disciples came slowly to grasp its spiritual nature. Just how slowly they caught on is revealed by their last question to the Lord: 'Lord, are you at this time going to restore the kingdom to Israel?' (Acts 1:6.)

Thus the apostle Paul was not coining a new concept when he included the word twenty-one times in his letters. In each case he alludes to a secret 'too profound for human ingenuity' according to Bauer's *Lexicon*. The entire gospel is labelled by Paul as a 'mystery hidden for long ages past' (Romans 16:25). The resurrection of believers also is classified as a mystery (1 Corinthians 15:51). Ephesians abounds with references to the 'mystery of Christ', the open secret of God's grace embodied in the Lord Jesus Christ (Ephesians 3:2-6). The church is a mystery explained by comparison with the marriage relationship (Ephesians 5:32). Varied as these references appear to be, they are united in their character. All explain divine truth which was concealed from the ancients and revealed through Christ.

One other New Testament book commands our attention; it is Revelation. In typically picturesque form, John records that 'the mystery of God will be accomplished' (Revelation 10:7). God's cosmic councils conceived in the eternal realms will surely come to fruition.

In each case, the New Testament application of the word 'mystery' stands out in sharp contrast with the ancient mystery religions. The pagans protected mysterious doctrines from the intrusion of common and ignorant folk. Only after long preparation could the novice undergo initiation into the temple, which was a repository of the secrets. In the New Testament 'mystery' was not a vehicle of secrecy but of revelation. These truths were broadcast by the coming of Christ and the sending of the apostles. God's mysteries are not closely guarded formulae but an open secret.

God's open secret

A climactic explanation of God's mystery is Colossians 1:27 where, under the inspiration of the Holy Spirit, Paul asserts that the long-hidden secret is now revealed to the saints. In turn believers are to broadcast this precious truth to the nations. In a word God's mystery is 'Christ in you, the hope of glory'.

God's mystery is a buttress against delusion by the imitations of the world, whether they originate in the apostolic or the aerospace age. Many modern pretenders to truth are strikingly similar to their ancient counterparts.

One characteristic of the early mystery religions was their limitation of truth to a select body. It was their mystery, and they guarded it as a primary weapon in their philosophical armoury. Only carefully selected individuals could intrude into the truth thus frantically held. Is that not also true today? The Mormons, for instance, cheerfully trudge from door to door seeking recruits. A superficial stratum of doctrine is offered to intrigue the gullible, the lonely and the untaught. Once won, however, the initiate is told of 'deeper truth', the rites which can only be accomplished in the temple. God's truth, by contrast, is offered openly to all who will read the Scriptures and permit the Holy Spirit to enlighten them.

A second aspect of the mystery religions was the nebulous, indefinite nature of their teaching. It was a mystical experience into which one entered. Truth, according to this party, is more often 'caught than taught'. Within Christianity, even within evangelicalism, we have many proponents of this theory. The important element in knowing God, they assert, is an emotional awareness of Him. Scripture is soon subjected to the judgement bar of experience. 'If it seems right to me, it is right,' these Christians insist. However, God's mysteries are revealed fully in the inspired pages of Scripture.

God's truth is not the property of an esoteric élite. The church of Jesus Christ never dare become possessive of God's open secret. It is not the property of a 'holy huddle', no matter how spiritual they seem to be. This dangerous élitism throughout history often has been concentrated in a priestly party. Before the Reformation Christians were excluded from exploring God's truth by both a linguistic and a liturgical barrier. The Bible was issued in Latin, safely out of reach of the plough-boy and the milkmaid. Furthermore, only the priest could understand and explain the Word. The clergyman had a monopoly on God; he had God in his pocket! Tyndale changed all this by risking the translation of the Bible into English. Needless to say, the clerical class was not amused. Never dare we lock up God's Word in the supposed safety of a theological cupboard. Paul was writing under inspiration when he exclaimed, 'I am suffering even to the point of being chained like a criminal. But God's word is not chained' (2 Timothy 2:9).

God's mysteries are revealed completely in the incarnate Christ. Charles Wesley had it right when he penned this famous hymn:

> 'Tis mystery all! The Immortal dies!
> Who can explore His strange design?
> In vain the first-born seraph tries
> To sound the depths of love divine!
> 'Tis mercy all! Let earth adore,
> Let angel minds inquire no more.

4.
Holy Spirit sealed

'Marked ... with a **seal**, the promised Holy Spirit' (Eph. 1:13)

The world is filled with marked men and women. From his birth Prince Charles was a marked person, destined for the throne. Others bear the marks of honour. One thinks of Sir Winston Churchill, whose very name is prefaced with a mark of respect. Infamy marks certain people, such as the notorious 'Jack the Ripper', or his modern counterpart, 'the Yorkshire Ripper'.

One may be a 'marked man' socially, but the Bible also speaks spiritually of 'marked people'. The apostle Paul described the Ephesian believers as those who are 'marked in him with a seal, the promised Holy Spirit' (Ephesians 1:13). Although Christians are not always noteworthy by human standards, they are noted by God.

The word used by Paul was a common expression in society, government and commerce. It is the Greek verb *sfragizo*, to seal. When a building was closed up, it was sealed. The secrets of the seductive Cleopatra were regarded as being sealed from the eyes of most mortals. Animals bore a seal, reminiscent of the sizzling branding iron of America's Wild West. Sacks of grain were sealed to indicate possession and the promise of ultimate payment.

Although the word was in common use, the apostle Paul elevated it to a very uncommon position. He declared that the Ephesian believers had been sealed when they believed. The verb is found here in the Greek aorist tense. This means that the action occurred in the past. The sealing has been completed.

It is also notable that all the believers were sealed. They

were marked with a seal when they believed. There appears to be no leakage here. All who believed were marked with the Holy Spirit as a seal, just as all those who believe are justified before God (Romans 5:1). Nowhere do we discover any indication of a two-tier Christianity. The Greek text flies in the face of anyone who suggests that there are 'normal' believers who have been saved by faith, and there are also 'super' saints who are 'sealed'. No such distinction is allowed by Ephesians 1:13.

The Spirit's seal is indispensable to the Christian's very existence. The Holy Spirit is God's agent in convincing people of their spiritual state apart from God (John 16:8-11). He it is who effects the new birth (John 3:5-6). In fact, no one can own Christ as Lord, unless the Spirit moves him (1 Corinthians 12:3).

Not only is this seal a necessary mark on all believers, it is also a guarantee of God's promises which are yet to be fulfilled (Ephesians 1:14). Just as God has promised a restoration of man and world, so He places within every believer a divine Guarantor. 'My word is as good as my bond,' the businessman used to say. God the Holy Spirit is the bond of His eternal Word, according to the Scriptures.

Having said that the Holy Spirit is the Guarantor of God's promises, we must indicate what this does not mean. It does not mean that the Holy Spirit is merely a pledge of fulfilment. When one signs a contract, one promises to pay, this is a pledge. When one pays the first instalment, one gives a guarantee of further payments. The Holy Spirit is the 'First Instalment' of heaven, and God will most certainly pay the remainder.

Signed, sealed and delivered

The thrust of these verses is the reliability of God. What He promises He is able to perform. He signed this contract in the blood of His only Son, the Lord Jesus Christ. He sealed the transaction with the Holy Spirit. Ultimately we shall take delivery in heaven. The uses of our word amplify and embroider its meaning.

The seal speaks of *security*. When the Lord was buried in Joseph's borrowed tomb, the cautious Jews wanted to prevent further incident. Thus He was sealed into the grave, and the Romans posted a military guard to prevent escape or grave-robbing (Matthew 27:62-66). The seal (v. 66) placed on the heavy stone door was to secure the tomb. One marvels at the extraordinary concern for keeping a dead man! Still a spiritual truth is seen in this use of the word 'seal'. We are sealed and thus secured by the Holy Spirit; His seal cannot be broken.

As already noticed, the seal is also a form of *identification*. In another place, Paul wrote to his problem children, the Corinthians: 'He anointed us, set His seal of ownership on us, and put His Spirit in our hearts as a deposit, guaranteeing what is to come' (2 Corinthians 1:22). A similar statement was sent to Timothy, when Paul reminded him that 'God's solid foundation stands firm, sealed with this inscription: "The Lord knows those who are his" ' (2 Timothy 2:19). God's mark on us is like the practice in modern agriculture. Not always is a brand burned into the cow's flank. Now a number is embossed there. The herdsman types that number into a computer, which displays instantly the milk production and the feeding requirements of each animal. God does not mark us with a number, but with His Holy Spirit. Nevertheless, He knows both our capabilities and our deepest needs.

A further meaning of the seal is *certification*. In John 3:33 we are reminded that the believer 'has certified that God is truthful'. The word translated 'certified' is actually our verb 'sealed'. In those ancient days when few could read, a seal certified the truthfulness of a document by imprinting a design on it. Most modern young people can read, but the seal is still used to certify their university diploma.

It is the commercial use of the seal which occurs in Ephesians 1:13-14. The seal is a *guarantee*. Writing to the Corinthians Paul said, 'God ... has given us the Spirit as a deposit, guaranteeing what is to come' (2 Corinthians 5:5). This reminds one of an engagement ring. Although born of a romantic attachment, the ring is a very serious symbol. It speaks of an existing love and prospective marriage. The symbol of promise will only come to fruition when the marriage is accomplished. Thus the Holy Spirit symbolizes the love of God and promises that we shall some day share in His glorious home.

Although the Spirit's sealing is primarily a source of comfort and joy, it is also joined to an admonition. In Ephesians 4:30 we are warned not to 'grieve the Holy Spirit of God, with whom you were sealed for the day of redemption'. Paul has enumerated some of the means by which Christians frustrate the Spirit: lust (v. 19), lying (v. 25), anger (v. 26), stealing (v. 28) and unwholesome talk (v. 29). Furthermore, Paul persists in warning them against anger and rage (v. 31).

The ever-present Holy Spirit is a spiritual light in our souls. He reminds us of the Lord who is the 'Light of the world'. Shining into dark corners, He turns up sin and sweeps it out. His illumination also enables us to comprehend the Scriptures and apply them to our lives. The Holy Spirit who seals us is this light, and He can be quenched. Thus the apostle wrote to the Thessalonians: 'Do not put out the Spirit's fire' (1 Thessalonians 5:19).

5.
Knowing God

*'That you may **know** him better'* (Eph. 1:17)

'It is not for the teacher, but for life that we learn,' claimed an Indian schoolmistress in the early years of our century. She saw that learning must be practical to be valuable. In this verse there is an eternal application of that principle.

Paul prayed that the Ephesians might 'know God better'. The verb 'to know' in this case is the Greek word *epiginosko*. It is a stronger form of the basic Greek word for knowing. Properly defined this strengthened verb means 'to know thoroughly'.

Paul directed this strong verb to the only valid object of our knowing: 'the God of our Lord Jesus Christ, the glorious Father'. From the apostle's standpoint, all of man's efforts must be directed to knowing God thoroughly. This becomes the 'magnificent obsession' of every saint. Something of this apostolic aspiration breathes from the pages of Tozer's *Knowledge of the Holy* and J.I. Packer's *Knowing God*.

In this lifelong effort the saint is not left to his own devices. God provides the means of attaining this essential knowledge. Paul reminded the Ephesians that God had given them 'the Spirit of wisdom and revelation' (v. 17). Individual Christians are thus not compelled to grope God-ward through cosmic darkness. The Holy Spirit 'extends His hand' to lead them into a deeper knowledge of God. Spiritual perception is a recurring theme in Pauline writings. To the Corinthians he wrote, 'The world through its wisdom did not know [God]' (1 Corinthians 1:21). But he assured them that God has freely given us His Spirit through whom we understand spiritual truth (1 Corinthians 2:10-15).

If the Holy Spirit is the source of spiritual truth, His 'wisdom and revelation' are the twin tools of working it out. Divine wisdom is bound up with knowing God and is received only as we contemplate Him with reverence (Proverbs 9:10). The concrete knowledge of God is in 'revelation', the revealed Word of God. It is the Holy Spirit who moved God's men to pen the sacred writings (2 Peter 1:21).

In the space of one brief verse the apostle adds it all up. Our aim in life is stated simply: 'to know God thoroughly'. The Holy Spirit is the infallible Guide into this essential knowledge. Into the hand of every believer are placed the tools: God's wisdom and revelation. Thus every believer is adequately equipped to enter upon this course of study.

Not just theory

Knowing God is a daunting task to all modern men, even to Christians. They are not quite sure where to start and what to do. It is a feeling of hopelessness and helplessness which overtakes them. I know this feeling, because it overwhelms me every time I peer at the engine of our car. The word we are studying, however, gives some valuable tips to the serious student of the Almighty. Within this word are represented three aspects of knowing God.

First the word implies *intimacy*. The apostle claimed in Romans 1:32 that mankind 'knew intimately God's righteous decree'. This speaks of detailed knowledge, a deep understanding, as pictured in marriage. The engaged couple know a good deal about one another. Basic facts such as favourite colour, hobbies and strong dislikes are accepted by the love-birds. How is he to know, however, that she squeezes the toothpaste tube from the middle and creates an intolerable situation? (Pardon my bias!) This is only known through the marriage relationship. This may even be the least unpleasant discovery of wedded bliss. Marriage means intimate knowledge. Our word speaks of this side of our relationship with God. With increasing deepness we learn to know God's divine desires.

The second aspect of this knowledge is *recognition*. During a recent visit to my home town in America I noticed a vaguely familiar person presiding at the church organ. Enquiries revealed that we had been contemporaries at college. Obviously time had done its destructive work on his hair and my waistline, but we still recognized one another. It is this 'knowing again' which is pictured in our word. We recall the couple on the road to Emmaus after Christ's execution (Luke 24:16-31). Only when He explained events in the light of prophecy and shared with them in a meal did they 'recognize' (know again) the Saviour. And they experienced a 'heartburn' of joy (Luke 24:32).

Finally, the word speaks of *acknowledgement*. In the Septuagint (Greek version) of the Old Testament, the word is used to characterize the reaction of Ruth to Boaz. 'Why have you "acknowledged" me, when I am a foreigner?' (Ruth 2:10, 19.) It is a reverse acknowledgement in Ephesians. The great is not acknowledging the small, but the penitent sinner saved by grace is acknowledging the 'glorious Father'. Like a knight bowing before the queen, we acknowledge God to be our infinite Sovereign. He dubs us not a knight of the realm but sons and daughters of the King of kings. How foolish we are if we do not devote all our efforts to knowing God!

A young lad spotted his aged grandfather poring over a well-worn Bible. 'Grandpa,' queried the boy, 'why are you studying the Bible so carefully?'

The old man's reply was direct: 'I am preparing for my final examinations!'

When all human wisdom fades away and human innovations are long since forgotten, only one kind of knowledge will remain. This is the knowledge of God. It is therefore necessary that we devote our best efforts to knowing God.

6.
Gathered church

'Head over everything for the **church***'* (Eph. 1:22)

The term 'ecclesiastical' produces instant gloom to many modern readers. It stirs up chilling memories of spooky old rectories which look like archetypal haunted houses complete with ghosts. On the other hand, some regard 'ecclesiastical' figures as comedy characters, bungling men in black suits and outmoded collars.

Actually the word 'ecclesiastical' deserves more serious treatment. It is derived from the Greek word *ekklesia*, usually translated 'church'. As a combination of two Greek words (*ek* — 'out' and *kaleo* — 'call'), *ekklesia* means those who have been called out. The New Testament applies it to a company of people whom God has called out of the world to fulfil His special purposes.

The book of Ephesians abounds with references to the 'church'. In Ephesians 1:22 it is viewed as a *powerful church*. Described as the Body of Christ, it is animated by His vibrant, eternal life. Just as the brain telegraphs impulses to the extremities of the body, so Christ directs and moves the Christians who make up His church.

Ephesians 2:19-22 reveals that the church is pre-eminently a *scriptural organization*. It is founded upon the two pillars of the prophets and apostles (Ephesians 2:20). Jesus Christ is the corner-stone, without whom the entire edifice crumbles. The final product is a temple to the worship of God. He fills this sanctuary with His Spirit as glory filled Israel's temple (Ephesians 2:22).

The church is also the instrument of God's revelation in history (Ephesians 3:10). It is a *triumphant church* which reveals the superiority of Christ over all authorities, human and superhuman. It almost propels us into the realms of science fiction, as we contemplate the conquest of demonic forces by our super Sovereign, the Lord Jesus Christ. The difference is that the spiritual conflict is fact.

After soaring into the stratosphere with Christ, we return to earth in Ephesians 4:11-16. Here is the effective church at work in the world. Taught by God-gifted teachers, the church is trained to penetrate the world with God's message. Again Paul portrays the church as a human body. Every member of the body must be active; no spiritual paralysis is tolerated. The object is 'works of service' (Ephesians 4:12), which the body performs for its edification and Christ's glory.

Finally in Ephesians 5:23-29 the *beloved church* is introduced. Like a wedding picture, the apostle paints a portrait of the church as Christ's much-loved bride. Lovingly she submits to Him in response to His absolutely sacrificial love. Out of this reciprocal relationship arises a unity which transcends both human understanding and also human history. It is a match made in heaven for eternity. The church is the bride chosen for the Lord Jesus Christ, who called her out of the world to be His own.

God's growing church

Throughout the New Testament the church is a recurrent theme. As the apostolic age unfolded, the concept gathered increasing significance and scope. There are four specific applications of the word 'church' in the New Testament.

The 'church' refers to the *meeting of believers*. To the Corinthian Christians Paul wrote, 'When you come together as a church' (1 Corinthians 11:18). He then proposed to chide them for divisions which marred the meeting. The fact remains that the meeting of believers is called 'church'. One of our children once asked, 'Daddy, why do we go to church every Sunday?' I explained that we went to worship the Lord and learn more about Him. We also saw our friends there and enjoyed fellowship with them. Going to church is a blessed, biblical habit for every sincere child of God.

A collection of all local Christians is also referred to as 'church'. Thus the thousands who turned to Christ at Pentecost became the 'church at Jerusalem' (Acts 5:11). Paul spoke of cells of converts scattered throughout the Mediterranean basin as glowing lights in a dark world (Philippians 2:15). When I was inducted to the pastorate at Bristol, a marvellous montage of churches was represented. Some came from small village chapels nestled in the countryside. Others represented great city churches towering as lighthouses over the tumult of social change. All were local churches composed of believers in their respective communities, and we share fellowship with them.

The New Testament refers to *house churches*. Priscilla and Aquila were outstanding examples of the godly family, who served as host and hostess to a house church (Romans 16:5). Wherever they went, their family approach to God's service was characteristic (1 Corinthians 16:19). I am reminded of a German lady who had lived in exile on the frontier in Russian Tashkent. In that remote region Christians frequently came together in homes, and not a few were banished to Siberia for this practice. These were biblical house churches — well taught, spiritually led and scripturally ordered. Now we hear that there are thousands of house churches in China.

A fourth application of the word is the *universal church*, all believers at all times in the entire world. To the Colossian Christians Paul wrote concerning the universal church which has Christ as its Head (Colossians 1:18). It is composed of those who have submitted to the Lordship of the Head, and it differs markedly from all other associations. For instance, a golf club chooses people with a certain sporting prowess. Academic associations are made up of those who demonstrate some intellectual ability. Social clubs are structured to provide appropriate amenities for men of financial capacity or social grace, or both. 'Wherever I go in the world there are members of my club', claimed a retired surgeon. 'They are all born-again members of Christ's Body.' Now that is an association with supernatural class!

The biblical church is a mind-boggler. It is composed of people from every race, social stratum and nationality. Without exception its members are evil by nature, but they are qualified by re-creation. Some have been dead for almost two millennia, and they are buried in the Roman catacombs. Millions of them have not yet been born. When taken together they comprise the church of Jesus Christ, and He has 'glory in the church throughout all generations' (Ephesians 3:21).

7.
Divine wrath

*'We were by nature objects of **wrath**'* (Eph. 2:3)

The wrath of God is a serious subject, and one introduces it only for therapeutic reasons. As a dentist must be 'cruel to be kind', so God's wrath is an instrument of His grace. Actually our English word 'wrath' is a translation of the Greek word *orgē*. It is transliterated in our word 'orgy', meaning uninhibited revelling and debauchery.

The wrath of God is a reasoned, providential phenomenon. Martyn Lloyd-Jones defines it as 'a manifestation of indignation based upon justice'. The wrath of God is 'nothing but the other side of the love of God'.[1] A similar approach is taken by William Hendriksen who sees God's wrath as 'settled indignation'. The wrath of God is not a divine temper tantrum, but the infinite indignation of a holy God against an irreparably fallen creation.

The Greek word for wrath occurs three times in Ephesians. In Ephesians 2:3 it describes God's attitude towards sinful people. Previously they have been described as being 'dead in transgressions and sins' (2:1). They habitually dance to the devil's tune (2:2), and they pattern their behaviour by the prevailing winds of the world (2:2). Motivation comes solely from their animal instincts and cravings which are untamed by divine grace and unleashed by sin (2:3). As they say, 'It's not a pretty picture.' It is the cause of God's wrath.

The second occurrence of our word is in Ephesians 4:31. There it is translated 'anger' as it characterizes Christians who are flying in the face of the Holy Spirit. Human anger lacks the settled, beneficial flavour of divine wrath. Therefore it is employed for the benefit of the angry person, rather than for the healing of its object. For this reason, the Christian who 'flies off the handle' grieves the Holy Spirit who lives inside him.

A third appearance of the word takes us back to divine wrath (Ephesians 5:6). It is demonstrated against those who disobey God. In fact, this disobedience is also reflected in Ephesians 2:2, where Satan is portrayed as the moving force in man's disregard for God's law. One could demonstrate that God's wrath is ultimately aimed at Satan and his henchmen in this world.

The wrath of God is not a manifestation of a violent, warlike deity hovering about with the intent of destroying the human race. Wrath is God's response to the sin which separates Him from His creature, the evil which made a mess of His perfect creation.

No way out

The wrath of God walls in the whole human race. No one can escape it, and the sentence is death. The most dramatic picture is the Berlin Wall which surrounds people and limits every activity. No escape is possible in theory, although some do fly the coop. From God's wrath there is only one way out, and God incarnate is that Door.

Actually there are three uses of the word 'wrath' in the Bible. The first is the human characteristic which we saw in Ephesians 4:31. It comes to the surface in James 1:20, where the apostle concludes, 'Man's anger does not bring about the righteous life that God desires.' Immediately our minds are filled with horrific visions. One sees the infant lying on the floor kicking his feet, flailing his arms and screaming until his normally cherubic little face is blue. Older children are capable of the same tantrums, but the result may be even more destructive when they kick a toy, or a piece of furniture, or a parent. In adulthood one expects a higher degree of civilization, but the angry horn-honking motorist weaves in and out of traffic intimidating the more normal drivers. He does not need to kick and scream; the horn and brakes do it for him. Anger at any age is the same, an expression of man's propensity to evil.

The second use of wrath is justified, because it is a characteristic of our holy God. We see His wrath in human history. When Adam and Eve turned their back on God and munched the forbidden fruit, they were expelled from Eden. At the entrance was stationed an angelic sentry with a flaming sword. He was a symbol of God's wrath. When Sodom and Gomorrah descended into the slime of debauchery, God's wrath rained down from heaven wiping out the cities. As Israel was drawn by the magnetic force of idolatry, Jehovah expressed His righteous wrath by unleashing upon them the Assyrian and Babylonian hosts. Their exile was a continuing reminder of God's wrath. To the Romans Paul wrote, 'The wrath of God is being revealed (in history) from heaven against all the godlessness and wickedness of men who suppress the truth by their wickedness' (Romans 1:18).

The third aspect of God's wrath is future judgement which will occur after human history is completed. The last prophet of Israel, John the Baptist, warned his contemporaries of the wrath to come (Matthew 3:7). The Lord warned of 'great distress ... and wrath against this people' (Luke 21:23). Implicit in Scripture is the teaching of a coming judgement. It is reflected also in human experience. Every schoolboy looks forward with anxiety to the inevitable school report. The good student is afraid that he will not maintain his usual standard, and the poor student is afraid of failure. The adult experiences the same feeling when a bill arrives in the letter-box. Weeks of carefree buying on the credit card are chastised by a bill. The evil in our world cries out for the justice of God, and His wrath will most surely be poured out upon the evil-doer who rejects Christ.

At the end of the New Testament one finds frequent references to God's wrath in the book of Revelation. One reads of sinful people pleading with the hills to hide them from God's wrath. Human rank and achievement melt like butter in the hot sun. Social distinctions cease to exist as the human race parades before God's bar of justice. The agent of

God's wrath is His Son, who suffered to spare man eternal damnation. He was offered like a sacrificial lamb to pay the penalty of man's sin, and this metaphor appears in Revelation as a reminder of His sacrifice. The cry of the condemned is this: 'Hide us from the face of Him who sits on the throne and from the wrath of the Lamb' (Revelation 6:16).

[1] D.M. Lloyd-Jones, *God's Way of Reconciliation*, p.51

8.
Free grace

*'By **grace** you have been saved'* (Eph. 2:5, 8)

Few Greek words are better known to the average English-speaking Christian than this one. The Greek word for 'grace' is *charis*, and we find it in English words such as 'charismatic'. Generally it refers to a person with unusual gifts, charm or presence, such as a politician with a 'charisma'. Religiously these words have become a battleground between the 'charismatic' and 'non-charismatic' Christians. In reality, all Christians are charismatic, objects of God's grace and recipients of God's grace-gifts.

Nowhere does the grace of God shine forth more brilliantly than in the book of Ephesians. Paul opens the letter with a greeting: 'Grace and peace to you from God our Father and the Lord Jesus Christ' (Ephesians 1:2). Some have thought he made a play on words substituting 'grace' (*charis*) for the normal Greek greeting, 'Rejoice' (*chaire*). The rest of Ephesians shows his deliberate emphasis on the grace of God.

Forgiveness is not earned by self-mortification, it is a gift of God's grace (Ephesians 1:7). In fact, the root meaning of 'grace' is 'to give freely'. So forgiveness is not bought but bestowed. It is God's free gift.

In Ephesians 2, Paul applies this word to our salvation. He introduces it in verse 5: 'By grace you have been saved.' This is expanded in verses 8-9: 'It is the gift of God — not by works, so that no one can boast.' Our relationship with God rests not upon our aspirations, but upon His free grace.

Collectively we demonstrate 'the riches of His grace' (Ephesians 2:7). A local church is a collection of people who, like shipwrecked seamen, have been snatched from sure death by divine grace. They are not supermen and women who swam to shore by their own strength. From the beginning God has been the sole saviour of mortal men and women, from the dying thief on the cross to the most recently converted child.

Not only is our salvation provided by grace, but we also serve the Lord through His grace. He gave us the skills for ministering to one another and to the world. The apostle Paul claimed, 'I became a servant of this gospel by the gift of God's grace given me through the working of his power' (Ephesians 3:7). The church is built by gifted people. The apostle Paul insists that 'to each one of us grace has been given as Christ apportioned it' (Ephesians 4:7). Just as we were saved and forgiven by grace, so God's grace equips us to serve the saints. These are not characteristics of temperament. (One thinks of one person with boundless energy and another exhibiting an unperturbed sense of calm.) Neither are they natural gifts, like the ability to perform music or the gift for public speaking. God's grace-gifts are bestowed by the Holy Spirit to build up God's church. Woe to the man or woman who perverts such gifts for his or her own self-glory! God will judge that person.

Paul concludes Ephesians with yet another reference to God's grace. He prays that God will give 'grace to all who love our Lord Jesus Christ with an undying love' (Ephesians 6:24). Just as God unilaterally pours out His grace upon people in salvation, forgiveness and enabling, so His pervading grace is seen in their lives.

We don't deserve it

According to the older theologians, grace is 'God's unmerited favour'. Someone else developed an acrostic definition: 'God's Riches at Christ's Expense'. These definitions share essential elements. God is the source of grace. His gifts are freely given. Those who receive them are totally undeserving. The word 'grace' is employed in the New Testament to cover a multitude of ideas.

First, it conveys the concept of *graciousness*. Even Christ's enemies were 'amazed at the gracious words that came from his lips' (Luke 4:22). Grace shone from the Saviour like light from a beacon. His speech was marked by God's grace. Therefore in Colossians 4:6 Christians are admonished: 'Let your conversation be always full of grace, seasoned with salt, so that you may know how to answer everyone.'

Second, *deeds* also reveal God's grace. Of the young lad Jesus we are told: 'He grew in wisdom and stature, and in favour (grace) with God and man' (Luke 2:52). The early Christians reflected their Lord, just as the moon reflects the sun. It could be said of them that they were 'praising God and enjoying the favour (grace) of all the people' (Acts 2:47). God's grace seen shining through His Son and His people is clearly evident, even to those who reject His grace.

Third, *salvation* is described as the grace of God in essence. Romans 6:14 speaks of Christians as those living 'under grace'. A corollary to this is Romans 5:2 where Paul speaks of gaining 'access by faith into this grace in which we now stand'. The entire scriptural revelation becomes in Paul's inspired mind 'the word of his grace' (Acts 20:32). Barnabas described the church at Antioch as a vivid illustration of God's grace (Acts 11:23). Salvation in all its aspects is seen as God's grace working among men, as yeast in the dough.

A fourth function of the word relates to *grace-gifts*. Already this has been seen in Ephesians 4:7. The parallel passage in Romans 12:6 speaks of the gifts we have 'according to the grace given us'. God not only creates His church out of depraved humanity, He also perfects it by the exercise of His grace. It is like the sculptor who has a piece of stone cut from the quarry and transported to his studio. Then he works with tools coarse and fine to produce the image which he saw in that stone. So God is at work transforming us by His grace into the image of Christ.

God's grace may be seen in another homely but helpful illustration. Our family dog, Inky, appears suddenly next to the table. She almost seems to have an instinct for our feeding time. When I sit down, the dear little mongrel takes up a statuesque pose at my right hand. Waiting in silence and innocence she hopes for a hand-out. Her thoughts must be these: 'If I am very good, perhaps that rather dull human will give me something.'

God's grace is just the opposite. Nothing which we can do will ever qualify us for His salvation. We cannot please God because we are flawed fatally by original sin. To us hopeless, helpless humans He gives salvation and all its attendant blessings. That is grace!

God's attitude towards us is variously described as mercy and grace. In mercy He withholds from us the punishment which His justice demands. By grace He gives to us the salvation and righteousness which we shall never deserve. 'Mercy pities. Grace pardons.' So we sing with John Newton,

> Amazing grace! how sweet the sound
> That saved a wretch like me;
> I once was lost, but now am found;
> Was blind, but now I see.

9.
Saving faith

'By grace you have been saved, through **faith,**
(Eph. 2:8)

Grace is a precise term, but faith is subjected to wildly sentimental perversion. 'I believe, for every drop of rain that falls,' croons the singer, 'a flower grows.' What growing flowers have to do with faith is not clear to the normal mind!

Screaming crowds of 'non-violent demonstrators' surged through the streets of America during the fifties and sixties. Their songs underlined their rabid resolve: 'We shall not be moved!' Slogans also hammered home their message: 'Keep the faith, baby!' To them faith meant a naive hope for a better future, a society hammered together with the scrap timbers of human aspiration.

Faith in the New Testament is much more meaningful than these examples indicate. In Ephesians 1:15 Paul thanks God for the Christians who were distinguished by 'faith in the Lord Jesus and ... love for all the saints'. Their commitment to Christ recognized fully His Lordship over their lives. It was also expressed in self-sacrificing love for other believers. Faith to the Ephesians was not a soft, sentimental belief in an unfounded optimism. It was firmly rooted in the divine Lord Jesus Christ.

Faith is wedded to God's grace in Ephesians 2:8. God acted unilaterally in providing for man's salvation. Nothing of which man was capable could compel God to save him. This is grace. Man grasps this amazing salvation by faith. Even faith, however, was a gift of God. God gave man the 'programme' of salvation. He beamed this to earth by His divine grace. Then He gave man the television set of faith to receive it. The availability of salvation only becomes meaningful when God gives the reception of faith.

Faith, according to Ephesians 3:12, gives us access to God in prayer. Jesus Christ has opened the door by providing redemptive reconciliation. He has not only swept away our sin, He has also satisfied God's justice. Therefore we can approach God. As Paul puts it, 'In Christ and through faith in him we may approach God with freedom and confidence' (Ephesians 3:12). Remember young John — John Kennedy. He marched into the President's White House office, because his father officiated there. So we can enter the throne room of heaven, where our Father is. His eternal Son opened the door for us.

Finally faith is Paul's parting blessing to the Ephesians. He uses Greek greetings, 'grace'. Also, he sometimes refers to the Jewish salutation of 'peace' (*shalom*). Here he reminds the Ephesians of all the pillars of their salvation: '*Peace* to the brothers, and *love* with *faith* from God the Father and the Lord Jesus Christ. *Grace* to all who love our Lord Jesus Christ with an undying love' (Ephesians 6:23-24). No thoughtless greeting is this; it reflects the doctrinal content contained in the entire letter.

Faith for living

Biblical faith is a veritable garden of spiritual hues and scents. Its meanings combine to excite the spiritual senses and attract the eye. Every aspect of faith is beautiful, none portrays a dark side. The Greek word to which we refer is *pistis*.

Faithfulness is the aspect of faith seen in human relations. We are told in Titus 2:10 that Christians are to 'show that they can be fully trusted'. They are to prove themselves 'faithful', full of faith. Men and women of faith are faithful men and women. This is evident in the marriage relationship, the commercial contacts and social interaction.

The root teaching about faith is directed towards God. Christians are those who *believe in the Lord*. As Bauer, the Greek scholar, puts it, 'God is specifically the object of the Christian's faith'.[1] There is a settled flavour about this faith, according to the hymn writer:

> My faith has found a resting place,
> Not in device or creed;
> I trust the ever-living One,
> His wounds for me shall plead.

Just as tall skyscrapers are built upon deep foundations reaching to the bedrock, so our faith rests upon the bedrock of God's grace.

Faith also speaks of *piety*. Paul writes to the Romans and commends them that their 'faith [is] being reported all over the world' (Romans 1:8). In the same passage he explains this faith as a standard of living: 'The righteous will live by faith' (Romans 1:17). Such a life of faith is seen in the example of Hudson Taylor, who risked the evangelization of China trusting solely in the Saviour. Like a tightrope walker he relied on only one safety net: God's provision. The result is the story of the Overseas Missionary Fellowship and the Chinese church, which has survived almost thirty years of enforced silence.

Another aspect of faith is the *virtue* which trusts God for the impossible. This is not the steady plodding faith of Hudson Taylor, but the bold belief of George Mueller. As I write, my study window looks out on a massive complex of buildings, the original Mueller homes. They were built by faith as George Mueller claimed the supply from God. Like the Christians at Corinth, Mueller 'excelled in faith' (2 Corinthians 8:7). Interestingly, he often met with Hudson Taylor and Charles Haddon Spurgeon for fellowship in their later years. What a concentration of faith that was!

Faith finally means a *body of doctrine*. The quiet little Epistle of Jude speaks of contending 'for the faith that was once entrusted to the saints' (v. 3). Christians mature spiritually as they grow in faith. Their comprehension of Bible doctrine is an excellent barometer of that growth. Faith is thus a body of doctrine. When it is neglected, it brings disaster. A professor in France had inculcated into his theological students false doctrine. Ruthlessly he destroyed their confidence in the

Scriptures. On his deathbed the professor repented and closed his eyes with this pathetic plea: 'Gather all my influence and bury it with me.' He had deserted the faith and now sought to return. Alas, for his students it was too late! He had forsaken the faith.

Faith and grace are wed in Ephesians 2:8. God provides salvation by grace without any human contribution. We cannot grasp this salvation by effort either. It is only by God-given faith that we are saved. Likewise our life must be marked by faith. To the Christian James writes, 'Faith by itself, if it is not accompanied by action, is dead' (James 2:17).

[1] Bauer, p.662

10.
Possible peace

'For he himself is our **peace***'* (Eph. 2:14)

In a world of festering feuds, peace appears to be an impossible dream. Conflict rages in the Middle East as Arabs and Jews attempt to gain advantage. There are many cases of civil strife, of which Ulster is a horrifying example. Within many industrialized nations one sees class conflict as labour and management compete for progressively larger slices of the profits.

Just as there are numerous examples of conflict, there are also various types of peace. There is the armed truce, when brother and sister glare at each other with clenched fists and teeth. 'I'm sorry,' they hypocritically spit out. There is also the total calm which characterizes a cemetery. It is a place of morbid peace, which the Germans call a *Friedhof* (peace yard). The peace which we find in the Scriptures is something else entirely. It is a quiet calm and sense of well-being in the face of turmoil and tempest, like the little bird sheltered in a nest within the cleft of a rock, while the rain and wind roar all around.

It is this peace to which Paul refers three times in Ephesians 2. The eternal source of our peace is none other than the Lord Jesus Christ: 'He himself is our peace' (Ephesians 2:14). It is no wonder that the prophet called Him the 'Prince of Peace' (Isaiah 9:6).

The practical expression of Christ's peacemaking is seen in His church. Jew and Gentile had for centuries been at loggerheads. The Jewish pride hoarded spiritual privilege, as a small child piles up sweets. Jews referred to Gentiles as 'dogs' and regarded all Gentiles, cultured or crude, as being beyond the pale. On the other hand, Gentiles hated the haughty Jews and hounded them throughout the known world. These humanly irreconcilable races were forged into one by the Prince of Peace. 'His purpose was to create in himself one new man out of the two, thus making peace' (Ephesians 2:15).

Not only was His character marked by peace and His work the source of peace, but Christ also brought a message of peace. When He was born, the angels sang, 'Glory to God in the highest, and on earth peace to men on whom his favour rests' (Luke 2:14). As His time drew near Christ gathered His men in an upper room. Calming them, He repeatedly assured them of His peace. He said, 'Peace I leave with you; my peace I give you. I do not give to you as the world gives. Do not let your hearts be troubled and do not be afraid' (John 14:27; 16:33). Because of this Paul could claim of Christ: 'He came and preached peace to you who were far away and to those who were near' (Ephesians 2:17).

Because the source of our salvation is an eternal peace initiative, the church is instructed to make peace. 'Keep the unity of the Spirit through the bond of peace,' Paul urges in Ephesians 4:3. Christians are to be peaceful people. The English word 'irenic' accurately reflects the Greek word for peace, *eirene*. Christians are to be irenic, those who are peaceful and aim to produce peace in all relationships.

Peace with justice

In 1952 Dwight Eisenhower ('Ike') became President of the United States. He inherited a war in Korea, and his primary aim was peace. The distinguished general set out immediately to create 'peace with justice'. In our day there is seldom either peace or justice.

Jesus Christ, however, achieved peace with justice nearly two thousand years before Eisenhower was born. First of all, Christ provided for us *peace with God*. The infinite, holy, just God was offended by man's sin. This produced a humanly unbridgeable gap. No matter how moral and upright man was, he invariably fell 'short of the glory of God' (Romans 3:23). The psalmist had concluded correctly, 'There is no-one who does good, not even one' (Psalm 14:3; 53:3). It was Jesus who came to our eternal rescue and assumed our sin, paid the penalty and paved the way to God (Romans 8:3-4). On the basis of this perfect sacrifice we can be acquitted at God's bar of justice: 'Since we have been justified through faith, we have *peace with God* through our Lord Jesus Christ' (Romans 5:1).

This peace with God leads logically to the *peace of God*. It is this peace which dominates our lives and our fellowship with other believers (Colossians 3:15). Paul also portrays this peace of God as a fortress. Christians are to be surrounded with the impenetrable walls of peace like a medieval fort. No care can thus breach these bastions, because 'the peace of God, which transcends all understanding, will guard your hearts and your minds in Christ Jesus' (Philippians 4:7).

Those controlled by Christ's peace are thus capable of creating peace among men. 'Blessed are the *peacemakers*,' Jesus proclaimed, 'for they will be called the sons of God' (Matthew 5:9). Christians, according to the apostle Paul, must 'make every effort to do what leads to peace and to mutual edification' (Romans 14:19). In fact, as far as they are able, Christians are to 'live at peace with everyone' (Romans 12:18). In the early sixties a noted speaker was called to preach at Birmingham, Alabama. Racial tension was at a fever pitch, and America was in a state of upheaval. The evangelist agreed to preach only if blacks and whites would be allowed to sit together. The colour barrier was breached, and a positive contribution to racial harmony was made. It is the gospel of Jesus Christ alone which can give lasting peace to our strife-torn society.

God's peace is not cheap. It was secured through the cross of Christ (Ephesians 2:13, 16). Maintaining the peace between believers is also not simple, it entails the crucifixion of self and the denial of personal desire. Peace is not easily achieved, but it is possible because of the Prince of Peace, the Lord Jesus Christ.

11.
Growing temple

'A holy temple in the Lord' (Eph. 2:21)

One cannot live in Britain without being impressed by magnificent churches and cathedrals, 'temples' to the Christian religion. As one approaches Salisbury, the cathedral steeple is seen soaring above the mundane dwellings of the city. In the heart of London one is moved to ponder eternal matters by the sight of St Paul's or Westminster Abbey, or the hundreds of parish churches and chapels. In Bristol we have the Church of St Mary Redcliffe, which Queen Elizabeth I regarded as 'the fairest, goodliest and most famous church in the kingdom'.

These churches are simply a sample of famous architecture. They were often built over a long period of time, and the builders viewed the effort as a service to God. Paul was also aware of impressive churches. He viewed the great temple at Jerusalem as the bastion of Judaism. In the pagan world he also knew the Ephesians' showpiece, their massive monument to Artemis (Diana). Subsequent archaeological investigations have revealed that the temple to Artemis was 390 feet long and 260 feet wide. One hundred columns stood around the temple supporting the ceiling 65 feet above. No doubt Paul was impressed by this lavish monument to idolatry.

Out of this understanding of temples Paul writes to the Ephesian Christians. After telling them that they are saved by grace through faith, he reveals the corporate nature of Christianity. They have been joined to a new international nation, the kingdom of God. Likewise, they have been born into a family which knows no loss through death, it is 'God's household' (Ephesians 2:19).

In Ephesians 2:20-22 Paul takes up a new metaphor for the church. It is a holy temple being erected to the glory of God. Its foundation is divine revelation. The apostles and the prophets have given to the church a firm basis of God's truth. The corner-stone upon which the church is built is none other than the Lord Jesus Christ (Ephesians 2:20). In fact, Paul told the Corinthians that 'no-one can lay any foundation other than the one already laid, which is Jesus Christ' (1 Corinthians 3:11).

Upon this foundation is erected a superstructure; it is a stone-walled building. Each stone is different, and every one fits. These are 'living stones' — individual Christians, according to 1 Peter 2:5. God, who dug them out of the quarry of sin, now shapes them by the sanctifying work of the Holy Spirit. They are 'joined together' according to Ephesians 2:21. That simple phrase 'joined together' translates a Greek word with two constituents: *syn* (as in *sym*phony sounding together) and *harmologeo* (as in harmony). Thus the Christians are 'brought together in harmony' to build God's temple. The temple is simply a building, however, apart from the presence of God by His Spirit. It is the Holy Spirit who gives life to believers individually and collectively. Then the temple resounds to the praise of God's people as the 'living stones' cry out in worship.

God's temple people

A few years ago there arose in California the 'People's Temple'. Led by the self-styled Rev. Jim Jones, it became a totalitarian cult. Ultimately the faithful moved to Guyana, where in 1979 their community collapsed, and more than 900 died in a grotesque suicide pact. What a travesty that was of the true temple of God's people!

Throughout the Scriptures there are many references to the 'temple', usually a translation of the Greek word *naos*. The idea of 'temple' in biblical terms arises first during the time of David, when he expressed the desire to erect a temple for Jehovah. Although David did not gain God's permission to build, his son, Solomon, did. The result was the fabulous temple at Jerusalem. Successive temples appeared in Jerusalem after the exile and during the reign of Herod. First, then, the word is used for the *temple at Jerusalem*.

A second use of the word is the *false temple* of Diana or Artemis. (Diana is the Latin form of the Greek Artemis.) This temple housed a fanatic worship of the goddess of fertility. When the gospel threatened that worship, the people rose up in a mass movement. They screamed non-stop for two hours: 'Great is Artemis of the Ephesians!' (Acts 19:34.) One is reminded of the radical Muslim revolutionaries in Iran when they surged in 1979 through the streets deposing the Shah and defying the United States. Such religious fervour, though false, fuels mass movements which are awesome in their scope. The Temple of Artemis was the recognized centre of such a fanatic movement.

Third, the *human body* is regarded as a temple. When viewing Herod's temple, the Lord Jesus Christ compared it with His own body. Prophesying His resurrection the Lord said, 'Destroy this temple, and I will raise it up again in three days' (John 2:19). The apostolic writer commented, 'But the temple he had spoken of was his body' (John 2:21). The Epistles also compare Christians' bodies to temples. They become temples by virtue of the Holy Spirit's presence in them (1 Corinthians 6:19).

What the believers are individually, they also are collectively. As God fits them together He forms a magnificent cathedral to His glory. They form a 'holy temple ... in which God lives by his Spirit' (Ephesians 2:21-22). God is no longer shut up to one temple or another. He is a Spirit who must have true spiritual worship, as Jesus said (John 4:24). Stephen tried to tell the Jewish leaders that God is not contained in temples, but they slew him rather than accept his assertion (Acts 7:48 ff). God is infinitely bigger than even the most magnificent cathedral. His true dwelling-place is the lives of men made new.

A fourth and climactic use of the word is seen in the rarified atmosphere of heaven, the *heavenly temple*. In Scripture we are told that the Lord God Almighty and the Lamb are the temple of the eternal Jerusalem. God alone stands as the focus for worship, and His hosts, angelic and human, gather around in a great *Gloria*.

What a contrast that eternal temple presents to the contemporary churches! One sees all around glorious cathedrals, but alas they are desecrated by commercialism and false teaching. Magnificent churches, too, are given over to the twin fallacies of ritualism and trendy theological innovation. Free churches were once gospel chapels, but now they vie with established churches for the favour of a fickle crowd. Many chapels, too, have been perverted by humanistic teaching totally foreign to biblical belief. All around we see humble little mission halls. Some have succumbed sadly to a lack of love and biblical teaching, and their sheet metal walls ring hollow.

One longs for the day when God's invisible temple takes on form. Together we shall share in the glory with our God, and a thousand magnificent organs shall stand silent as the saints sing, 'Worthy is the Lamb!'

12.
The revealing God

'The mystery made known to me by **revelation***'* (Eph. 3:3)

'Is this dress too revealing?' I remember a relative asking some years ago. In other words, 'Does it leave too much of me uncovered?' 'To uncover' is the root meaning of the biblical word 'to reveal'.

The Greek word for 'revelation' is *apocalypsis*. It is accurately reflected in such English terms as 'apocalypse' and 'apocalyptic'. Usually these refer to the dramatic revelation of God's power at some future date, at the end of the world. The book of Revelation (The Apocalypse) has coloured our understanding of the word.

Really, the word 'revelation' has a much broader application in the Bible, especially in the Ephesian Epistle. The knowledge of Christianity is mediated to the believer by the 'Spirit of wisdom and revelation' (Ephesians 1:17). We shall never catch on to spiritual truth through the straining of our puny reason, but only through the aid of God's revelation.

The other references to 'revelation' appear in the third chapter of Ephesians, in the portion mentioned above. The 'mystery of Christ' has been revealed by the incarnation of Christ. When He broke into the rat-race of human history, He revealed God in a personal, powerful way. The 'mystery of Christ' is a Pauline synonym for the whole gospel (Ephesians 3:3-4).

The agents of revelation are 'God's holy apostles and prophets' (Ephesians 3:5). God hid this truth of Christ from previous generations, although He gave certain prophetic clues. Like a dedicatory plaque on a new building, God's truth was covered up until the 'unveiling'. The Greeks used the word *apocalupto* (to uncover). God has now uncovered the secret of His salvation and showed it to His apostles and prophets. Incidentally, the prophets and apostles seem to be identical (cf. Ephesians 2: 20; 4:11).

According to the apostle Paul, an 'apocalypse' has occurred. The revelation to which he referred is the message God commissioned him to preach. Paul's revelation forms the basis of evangelism and edification for the church at Ephesus, and indeed all churches since then.

Taking the lid off

God has uncovered His eternal plan for man's redemption. In a word, that plan is Christ. He is that 'great light' which was envisaged in Isaiah 9:2 and sighted by first-century Jews (John 1:4-5) and Gentiles (2 Corinthians 4:6). His light pierced the blackness of our world and personified God's revelation. In the New Testament 'revelation' has four distinct meanings.

First, 'revelation' refers to Bible *truth* in general. Simeon, the saintly old priest, understood immediately that the infant Christ was 'a light for revelation to the Gentiles and for glory to your people Israel' (Luke 2:32). It took well-honed spiritual insight to see this, and Simeon's decades of divine service had prepared him admirably.

In Romans 16:25 Paul returned to his theme of mysteries revealed. In Christ God points out that 'mystery hidden for long ages past'. Mysteries were insights apprehended only by divine help and the mystery of the gospel required the crowning touch of all revelations, the appearance of the Messiah, the Lord Jesus Christ.

Recently we were walking with friends in the Herefordshire hills. As we started our descent, we left the marked path. Impatiently I forged on ahead, hearing the voices of my family and friends shouting, 'Where are you?' My companion held up a stick and replied, 'We are here! Follow us!' Similarly, while we were lost in the maze of sin, Christ was lifted up on a tree and called, 'Follow me out of the maze!' That is the genius of revelation.

A second meaning of 'revelation' is more specific, the *prophetic word* concerning future events. Throughout the Old Testament prophecy pointed to the coming of Christ. In the New Testament Christ is the channel of revelation. The apostles wrote of visions and revelations from the Lord Jesus Christ (2 Corinthians 12:1; Galatians 1:12). He overshadowed all other revelatory vehicles throughout the New Testament. The future will reveal Christ in all His glory (1 Peter 4:13).

There is progress in biblical revelation. In nature we see the relentless revelation of God. Violate God's revelation in nature, and you will pay the penalty. If you step over a precipice you will fall, no matter how sincerely you repent (Romans 1:20). When revelation appeared in the Old Testament there was yet another aspect of divine truth. The law of God had verbal content; God spoke in words we could understand. That we understood them, however, did not mean that we could keep them. In fact, Paul taught that the law gives us only an understanding of our failure (Romans 3:20). As a petrol gauge reveals our need of petrol but adds nothing to the tank, so the law shows our sinfulness without adding any virtue. Beyond the revelation of nature and the law, we see the perfect revelation of Jesus Christ. He is God's last word to a sinning human race (Hebrews 1:3). In Him we see truth wedded to grace, whereby God gives us the ability to stand before His justice (John 1:17-18).

Third, the New Testament speaks of the *revelation of believers*. From the outset of creation, the world has been in suspense waiting 'for the sons of God to be revealed' (Romans 8:19). When the apostle John wrote his first Epistle, he was guided by the Spirit to prophesy that 'when He [Christ] appears, we shall be like Him, for we shall see Him as He is' (1 John 3:2). 'What a gathering of the ransomed that will be!'

Continually people parade to fortune-tellers in pursuit of their future. Apart from the satanic power conveyed by such practices, there is a high degree of improbability concerning fulfilment. The prophecy of the Bible about believers, however, is as reliable as the Lord of revelation.

Fourth, the final use of the word is '*the revelation of Jesus Christ*' (Revelation 1:1). In this remarkable, unique New Testament prophetic book, one sees the ultimate triumph of the Lord Jesus Christ. Although many simply write it off as a symbolic statement, there are certain elements of doctrinal truth implicit in it. The final victory of Christ over Satan gives us courage. The ultimate glorification of the church confirms our belief in the rest of New Testament truth. The irreversible condemnation of Satan agrees with the earliest of all prophecies (Genesis 3:15). Heaven is presented as the home where all believers will dwell with their living, reigning Lord. There no tears, terrors or temptations will molest the Christian.

To discuss revelation in so few words is presumptuous, and one is left with the impression expressed by the Queen of Sheba when she saw Solomon: 'Not even half was told me' (1 Kings 10:7).

13.
Spiritually rich

'To preach ... the unsearchable **riches** *in Christ'* (Eph. 3:8)

A recent popular commentary on Ephesians bears the tital *Be Rich*. In it the American preacher, Warren Wiersbe, tabulates the riches available to believers in Jesus Christ. In his author's preface Dr Wiersbe summarizes, 'Too many Christians are living like paupers when Christ has made us rich! Isn't it time we stopped living on substitutes (even *religious* substitutes) and started drawing on the riches we have in Christ?'

The Greek word for 'rich' is *ploutos*. When one studies the New Testament, it appears that Paul had a monopoly on its use. There are twenty-two occurrences in the New Testament, and fifteen of them are in Pauline Epistles. The Greek word has also found its way into English, and it is visible in such words as 'plutocracy' and 'plutocrat'. This speaks of the rule of the rich. Paul takes great pains to prove that we who believe in the Lord Jesus Christ are spiritual 'plutocrats'. We have spiritual wealth and we shall rule and reign with our Lord in His kingdom.

Ephesians is especially full of references to the riches we possess. Our *past* sins are forgiven according to the 'riches of God's grace' (Ephesians 1:7). From God's standpoint, the Christian has no 'skeletons in his cupboard'. All of them have been disposed of, and the measure of this deliverance is 'the incomparable riches of his grace' (Ephesians 2:7).

If the believer's past is purged, his *present* is marked by supernatural power. Paul prayed for the Ephesian saints: 'That out of his glorious riches he may strengthen you with power through his Spirit in your inner being' (Ephesians 3:16).

Christians are men and women who have their feet firmly planted on the earth. They are not spared from sickness, suffering and death. Neither do they escape the 'caprices' of natural, economic and political disasters. The only difference is their source of spiritual power — God's 'glorious riches'.

Not only is the past forgiven and the present provided for, the *future* also is secured. If this were dependent on human effort, it would be a presumptuous pretence. The ultimate destiny of the Christian lies in the hands of his God. At the outset of his letter, Paul reminded the Christians that they looked forward to 'the riches of his glorious inheritance in the saints' (Ephesians 1:18). Not only is the Lord the treasure of His people. The apostle indicates that God's people are His treasure, too. This inheritance is potentially ours, and when we see Him our legacy will be paid out in full, and more!

This storehouse of spiritual wealth provides for our past, present and future, and it is summed up in Ephesians 3:8. There Paul admits that he is 'less than the least of all God's people'. Nevertheless God's grace enabled Paul to 'preach the unsearchable riches of Christ'.

Poor rich man

It was Noel Coward who wrote the song about a 'Poor Little Rich Girl'. The gist was this: money without happiness and love does not make one rich. To put it in the words of wise old Solomon: 'Better a little with the fear of the Lord than great wealth with turmoil' (Proverbs 15:16). The subject of riches runs throughout the Scriptures.

In the Old Testament, riches are viewed as a *mixed blessing*. The patriarchs regarded wealth as a mark of divine approval. When he met Esau after years of strained relations and the resultant separation, Jacob gave this testimony: 'God has been gracious to me and I have all I need' (Genesis 33:11). Very soon after settling in the promised land, however, the Jews began to experience the danger of wealth. The very wealth with which Jehovah had endowed them soon became a stumbling-block to their faithfulness. The great king Solomon warned them, 'Whoever trusts in his riches will fall, but the righteous will thrive like a green leaf' (Proverbs 11:28).

The abiding truth of this proverb is evident in our world. How often does material wealth lead to spiritual poverty! A saintly old Belgian army chaplain once told me, 'Money is a great servant, but it is a terrible master.'

It is the *danger of riches* which is emphasized by New Testament writers. Paul, who praised spiritual wealth, also condemned dependence on material goods. In writing to young Timothy, Paul said, 'The love of money is a root of all kinds of evil' (1 Timothy 6:10). The aim was warning, lest Timothy be ensnared in the quagmire of greed. Further, Paul urged Timothy to teach Christians the instability of money: 'Command those who are rich in this present world not to be arrogant nor to put their hope in wealth, which is so uncertain, but to put their hope in God who richly provides us with everything for our enjoyment' (1 Timothy 6:17). The axiom is this: if we rely on riches we shall be let down. If we trust in the Lord we shall have both spiritual and material security. God never promises excess, but He does promise sufficiency. Therefore we hold our possessions in an open hand, knowing that what we give to the Lord will be amply repaid.

It is not material riches which are commended in the New Testament, but *spiritual wealth.* To the Romans Paul wrote, God made 'the riches of his glory known to the objects of his mercy, whom he prepared in advance for glory' (Romans 9:23). The abundant blessings which we receive in time and space are simply samples. The real thing will only be evident when we are with Him in the glory. Now we have only a small sample. Recently we looked at little bits of carpet. Some showed pictures of rooms covered with that particular pattern. But it was only when our lounge was carpeted with that lovely warm fabric that the full impact was felt. God gives us little examples of His riches here and now. When we are with Him, however, the full expanse will be seen and appreciated. For we shall then, and only then, have the capacity to take it in.

To the Colossians Paul taught another aspect of spiritual riches. Those Asian believers were given by God's grace 'the full riches of complete understanding, in order that they may know the mystery of God, namely, Christ' (Colossians 2:2). Here *spiritual knowledge* is portrayed as a treasure. When the truth of Christ dawns on believers they are enriched immeasurably. This is clear to us when we consider the education of children. When children learn to read they are introduced to all sorts of new things. One remembers how they read the street signs, the cereal packets at breakfast, and all those things long since ignored by adults. As they grow towards maturity they are introduced to the treasures of their language and the wisdom of the ages. Christian parents quickly lead their little ones to read the greatest of all books, the Bible. Through reading God's Word the little ones come to see their need and claim Christ as their Lord. This is certainly the greatest boon available to man, woman and child.

It is the spiritual blessing which is true wealth. Material possessions are constantly under attack. Inflation saps the bank account of value. Decay attacks the car, house and other things. Sickness and death even rob one of priceless health. But God's goodness gains in value even when we cross the frontier of death and enter eternity. Small wonder that Solomon, who had both inherited and earned wealth, wrote, 'The blessing of the Lord brings wealth, and he adds no trouble to it' (Proverbs 10:22).

14.
Many-splendoured wisdom

'The manifold **wisdom** *of God'* (Eph. 3:10)

To the philosophical Greeks, wisdom was the ultimate fascination. They gave birth to the word 'philosophy', and it summarized their obsession: *phileo* means 'to love', and *sophia* is 'wisdom'. The Greeks 'loved wisdom', no matter what the source. They were 'philo-sophers'.

When the apostle Paul reached Athens, he found robust Athenian men sitting around listening to new ideas. 'All the Athenians and the foreigners who lived there spent their time doing nothing but talking about and listening to the latest ideas' (Acts 17:21). We do not know much about the women, but the Athenian men were certainly great talkers and listeners.

It seems as though the Ephesians, too, were preoccupied with 'wisdom'. The apostle capitalized upon this interest to teach spiritual truth. From the outset, Paul presented the principle that wisdom originated with God alone. In the appearance of Christ, God's grace was 'lavished on us with all wisdom and understanding' (Ephesians 1:8).

Even though God revealed His wisdom in Christ, the Ephesians would never have grasped it without supernatural help. Their best philosophers and the most skilled proponents of logic would not have discovered divine truth. It was only through 'the Spirit of wisdom and revelation' (Ephesians 1:17) that they comprehended spiritual truth. Wisdom is more than understanding and larger than knowledge. Michel de Montaigne, the French essayist, concluded, 'We can be knowledgeable with other men's knowledge, but we cannot be

wise by other men's wisdom.' The only true source of wisdom
is God's Holy Spirit.

To the Ephesians, then, Paul taught one elementary truth
about wisdom: its sole source is divine and its complete
content is Christ. A modern definition of wisdom has been
attempted by all sorts of Bible teachers. Martyn Lloyd-Jones
described the wisdom of God as 'that attribute by which He
arranges His purposes and His plans, and arranges the means
which bring forth the results that He purposes'. The
American preacher and philosopher of Christianity, A.W.
Tozer, said it even more simply: 'Wisdom ... is the ability to
devise perfect ends and to achieve those ends by the most
perfect means.' It is this divine wisdom which the church
demonstrates to the world, and to the angels (Ephesians
3:10).

Ways and means

In American Congress there is an almost omnipotent body
called the 'Ways and Means Committee'. It is they who
smooth the path of legislation through the House. These men
can literally make or break a law before it even starts its
perilous passage.

Wisdom, in biblical terms, describes the ways and means
by which God's plans are brought to fruition. The New
Testament contains applications of the word 'wisdom'.

First, the *inadequacy of human wisdom* is portrayed in the
Bible. The classical statement of wisdom is Solomon's
collection of proverbs. In Proverbs 3:7 the reader is warned
against being 'wise in your own eyes'. True wisdom is found
outside human experience (Proverbs 3:13). The apostle Paul
approached this subject in his introduction to 1 Corinthians:
God will 'destroy the wisdom of the wise' (1:19). A contrast is
presented between 'human wisdom' and 'words taught by the
Spirit' (1 Corinthians 2:13).

When human wisdom seeks to trace God's ways, it becomes
hopelessly lost. When a loved one falls victim to an incurable
disease, human wisdom seeks scientific or human reasons and

comes up against a wall of silence. A baby is snatched away by death, and the only comfort is a fatalistic phrase: 'One baby in a thousand dies.' When the firm closes down and a lifetime of occupational skills is flushed down the drain, there appears to be no human answer but a 'golden handshake'. Somehow it is not enough to brew up a cup of tea and whisper, 'Never mind, love!' Human wisdom is dreadfully limited.

A second use of 'wisdom' in the New Testament is the description of people with *spiritual wisdom*. Wise Solomon had concluded, 'The fear of the Lord is the beginning of wisdom' (Proverbs 9:10). The Lord promised the disciples that He would give them 'words and wisdom' that none of their enemies could withstand (Luke 21:15). When the church came to select the seven deacons in Acts 6, they were described as men 'known to be full of the Spirit and wisdom' (Acts 6:3). Spiritual wisdom is imparted by God to people He chooses to use. The great biblical scholar, Richard C. Trench, spoke of this: 'There can be no wisdom disjoined from goodness.' Spiritual wisdom gives a quality of life foreign to mundane men.

Third, the centre of divine wisdom in human history was *God's redemptive work in Christ.* Jewish religious leaders expected a politically potent Messiah, and they stumbled over Christ. Greeks could not conceive of a Messiah who was not a philosopher, and they discarded Him as a rustic religious leader. But believers discovered Christ to be the 'wisdom of God' (1 Corinthians 1:24). Here is the genius of wisdom: God's perfect end (salvation) pursued by God's perfect means (Christ).

One can scarcely comprehend this sort of wisdom. It is like a child studying an intricately printed circuit. The silver symmetry is fascinating. The flow of an electrical charge works. The essence of the circuit is totally beyond the child's ability, and that of most adults. God's saving plan for man is beyond the reach of man's mind; only divine wisdom can open our eyes.

Fourth, Christ not only was the agent of divine wisdom, He

was the *personification of divine wisdom*. Paul stated this when discussing the limits of human wealth and wisdom. In 1 Corinthians 1:30 Paul asserted, 'Christ Jesus, who has become for us wisdom from God'. To the Colossians he similarly said, in Christ 'are hidden all the treasures of wisdom and knowledge' (Colossians 2:3).

In 1976 the United States celebrated its 'bi-centennial', two hundred years of independence. In a marvellous gesture, Queen Elizabeth II visited the country. The Americans, whose ancestors treated Crown representatives so shamefully in the eighteenth century, welcomed the queen in a befittingly royal fashion. The Yankees were ecstatic in their reception. She symbolized for them not only a gracious lady, but Britain itself. In an infinitely greater degree Christ came to earth. To a people who had sinned for centuries the Creator became incarnate and revealed the wisdom of God. Through the Holy Spirit's enlightening and God's sovereign calling, men and women received Him. Now they have God's gracious invitation: 'If any of you lacks wisdom, he should ask God, who gives generously to all' (James 1:5).

15.
Super love

*'This **love** that surpasses knowledge'* (Eph. 3:19)

One modern author defined love as 'a word used to label the sexual excitement of the young, the habituation of the middle-aged, and the mutual dependence of the old'. Love, according to that cynic, is simply an accommodation to men's basic drives.

But the Bible portrays another kind of love. It is as different from humanistic love as Concorde is from a kite. Biblical love is portrayed by the Greek word *agape*. It is distinguished by its totally altruistic motive: love for what it can give, not for what it can get.

Ephesians abounds with references to this sort of *agape* love. God's love is described with this term. 'In love he predestined us to be adopted as his sons,' according to Ephesians 1:4-5. Although we were stubbornly and congenitally rebellious towards God, He touched us with His mercy 'because of his great love for us' (Ephesians 2:4). God's love is seen as a motive for His redemptive intervention in human history. No intrinsic value attracted Him to us; it was solely an expression of His love.

Because Christians are objects of God's love, they are capable of expressing that love. In fact, the Ephesians were renowned for their 'love for all the saints' (Ephesians 1:15). Parental love grows with the addition of each baby to the family, and Christians' love expands to embrace all the Christians they know. Thus Paul can speak of a love as large as God's family.

Ephesians contains two references to the multiplying nature of God's love. In Ephesians 5:1-2 Christians are exhorted to 'live a life of love'. The motive for this is Christ, who 'loved us and gave himself up for us'. Children who know love become adults capable of showing love, but those who are denied parental affection are often incapable of loving. Thus a Christian who has experienced first-hand the love of the Lord cannot help but show it to others.

The climactic picture of God's love is Ephesians 3:17-19. Paul prefaces his statement by urging the Christians to be 'rooted and established in love' (Ephesians 3:17). Two pictures are presented. As a mighty oak sends sturdy roots to the water table, so a Christian is to plunge his roots deep into love. Love will then flow through his spiritual life producing appropriate fruits of Christian character. The second picture is also applicable. The Christian is to be 'established' or founded on love. As a building is supported by its foundation, so the Christian life must rest firmly on love. When love fails, the façade of Christianity soon cracks.

Having thus spoken of our love, Paul buttresses it by a classic statement of God's love in all its dimensions (Ephesians 3:18). It is a *broad love* capable of embracing every social class, national group, intellectual stratum and racial shading. No one is beyond the breadth of God's love. It is likewise a *long love*. Children soon tire of a new puppy or goldfish. Marriage partners often outgrow one another and cast around for some new 'playmate'. Parents sadly sometimes disown their own flesh and blood. But God's love is as long as eternity. Nothing shall separate us from the love of God (Romans 8:39). The love of God is also a *high love*. Certainly the truth of the incarnation is this: Christ came down from heaven so that we may go up to glory. God's love extends to heaven making room for the repentant believer there. Finally, the love of God is a *deep love*. It sent the Son of God to the depths of the cross. Imagine the God of all in human flesh being beaten, mocked, laughed at, spat upon. Because of His humiliation, savlation is open to the lowest of all human forms. He is able to 'save to the uttermost'. No one is beyond the ability of God's grace and election. The dimensions of God's love are far greater than a puny paragraph, but the Holy Spirit will expand our vistas.

Asked about the most profound thought he had ever had, one noted theologian recently said, 'The most profound thought ever to cross my mind is this: "Jesus loves me, this I know, for the Bible tells me so." '

Love that works

God's love is an efficient force in shaping saints. According to 1 Corinthians 8:1, 'Knowledge puffs up, but love builds up.' Or to put it in the words of Oliver Cromwell's chaplain, Stephen Charnock (1628-1680): 'What is in the Word a law of precept, is in the heart a law of love.'

The word *agape* is used first to describe *human love* supercharged by God's Spirit. The classic statement of such love is 1 Corinthians 13. It is a love which is patient, and never blows up. No green-eyed envy discolours this love. Neither is there any hint of boasting in either the quality or the object of this love. This love is never rude, remembering that Christ was always a gentleman. It never looks out for its own interests. 'Number One' is demoted to last place. It keeps no record of insults. Never does the person motivated by God's love say, 'I may forgive, but I shall never forget.' Such love characterizes the one who is under the Spirit's control.

This love reminds me of a lady I once knew on the south coast of England. She was converted from a life of profanity and hatred to the Lord Jesus Christ. She immediately began to witness to her husband, but he answered with abuse both verbal and physical. Years passed before he finally capitulated to the love of God as he saw it in his wife. His remaining days were radiant with the Lord's presence, and she finally saw him go on ahead to glory.

A second aspect of *agape* love is the *love of God for man*. Certainly John 3:16 must be the primary passage dealing with this love. God loved the world. God gave His Son. God saves believers. When Martin Luther's Bible was being printed, the printer's daughter found a scrap bearing the words: 'God so loved that He gave.' The little one asked her mother what God gave, and the mother's wise answer was this: 'I do not know what God gave, but if He loved us enough to give anything, we can trust Him to give us the best.' We are reminded by the apostle Paul, that God's love was demonstrated to us 'while we were still sinners' (Romans 5:8). Deserve it we did not, but we shall have eternal profit from His love.

Third, God is not only the Communicator of *agape* love, *He is love*. The beloved apostle John was most frequently the expositor of God's love. In 1 John 4 we are repeatedly reminded of this essential love. 'God is love' is stated in verses 8 and 16. In verse 18 we are told that God's 'perfect love drives out fear'. As light expels the darkness from a closet, so God's love penetrates every corner of our lives driving out fear. This is especially pertinent when considering eternal punishment. Because God loves us, we have no more fear of judgement. Charles Haddon Spurgeon, the Victorian 'Prince of preachers', put it this way: 'God soon turns from His wrath, but He never turns from His love.'

There is a fourth aspect of this love, the *love of God for Christ*. The selfless aspect of this love is difficult to understand from a human standpoint, but the divine implication is impossible to grasp. In John 15:9 the Lord spoke of the love of the Father for His Son. This is the pattern for Christ's love towards us. Colossians 1:13 describes Christ as the 'Son whom [God] loves', and Ephesians 1:6 calls Christ 'the One [God] loves'. It was Augustine, I think, who devised a proof of the Trinity predicted on God's love. His argument runs like this. God is love. God is eternally unchangeable. Therefore, God must have had an eternal object of His love: Christ. (Although this does not necessarily demonstrate the Trinity, it does demonstrate plurality in the Godhead.)

Like a mountain stream, God's love arises in the peaks of His nature. It flows down through the forest and waters the valley. All the rivers of human love have their ultimate source in His love.

16.
Full-filling God

*'Filled to the measure of all the **fulness** of God'* (Eph. 3:19)

Recently a television programme was transmitted from a submarine at sea. The diving and surfacing manoeuvres fascinated me. On the command to dive certain chambers were filled with water and the ship slipped beneath the waves. When commanded to surface the submarine expelled the water by forcing air into the same compartments. When they were filled with water the submarine submerged; when air expelled the water the craft surfaced.

It is this concept of filling to which Paul refers. The Greek word he uses is *plēroma* (fulness), and the verb form for 'filling' is *pleroō*. 'Fulness' in the Bible usually relates to the greatness of God, and the apostle Paul makes frequent use of this concept. Ephesians is one of his prime showcases for the 'fulness of God'. 'Fulness' refers to completion, where nothing further is needed.

In Ephesians 1:23 we are reminded that Christ as Head of the church 'fills' His body. In fact, the church is characterized by 'the fulness of him who fills everything in every way'. The presence and power of the living Lord penetrate into every corner of His church. No member of the universal church of Jesus Christ is excluded from the presence of Christ. As light illuminates a dark room, so the Saviour pierces into every corner. He 'fills everything in every way' in His church.

Although every believer is touched by Christ's fulness, the apostle prays that each Ephesian Christian 'may be filled to the measure of all the fulness of God' (Ephesians 3:19). Christians must allow the fulness of God to reach into all aspects of their lives. Thoughts are filled with Christ, and this is called the renewing of one's mind (Romans 12:2). Doubts which cause unbelievers to stumble at the gospel are usually swept away when one is converted. Emotions are also filled by the fulness of God. Bitter hatred of a parent can be transformed into love by the fulness of Christ. The will of man is also filled by God, as one experiences that fulness of the knowledge of God's will (Colossians 1:9). The fulness of Christ in the believer was stated most clearly by Augustine: 'Thou hast created us for Thyself, and our heart cannot be quieted till it may find repose in Thee.'

The fulness of the Lord is also seen in Ephesians 4:10, where He is shown to be the One who 'fills the whole universe'. God is omnipresent. There is nowhere where he is not. An atheist scribbled on a scrap of paper: 'God is nowhere'. His believing daughter rearranged the letters: 'God is now here.' To every believer the fact of God's omnipresence is abundantly and comfortingly clear.

Maturity in the Christian life is also related to the fulness of the Lord. Christians attain to maturity in the faith as they experience 'the whole measure of the fulness of Christ' (Ephesians 4:13). Here the emphasis lies in being complete. As one's experiential knowledge of the Lord becomes more complete, one approaches maturity in the faith. It is interesting to note that such spiritual maturity is presented in the Scriptures as an achievable goal. Obviously it does not imply either sinless perfection or total comprehension of all spiritual truth. This must wait until we 'know fully, even as I am fully known' (1 Corinthians 13:12).

A final reference to 'fulness' occurs in Ephesians 5:18, when readers are enjoined to be 'filled with the Spirit'. This command is presented in the present, progressive tense and can thus be translated: 'Be continually filled with the Spirit.' Baptism by the Holy Spirit is simultaneous with conversion, as is the sealing of the Spirit (Ephesians 1:13). This viewpoint is disputed, of course, by some preachers and scholars. The filling of the Spirit's power is a continual action. In the Old Testament it was enabling for a special task, an unusual example of which is the equipment of the craftsmen Bezalel and Oholiab for work on the tabernacle (Exodus 35:31, 34). After Pentecost, however, all believers had the Holy Spirit and the possibility of being filled with Him. There is a comfort in this teaching concerning God's fulness. No matter what our lot, God is able to fill the gap. He is infinitely able to cope with the crises of our lives. This brings glory to God 'in the church and in Christ Jesus' (Ephesians 3:21).

God-sized measure

In the New Testament our word *plēroma* (fulness) has several distinct meanings, most of which closely parallel our English usage. The key concept is completion: what is fulfilled is completed without any gap.

First, the word pertains to *contents*. The disciples had been fishermen, so the Lord used images familiar to them. The kingdom of heaven is likened to a drag-net full of all kinds of fish (Matthew 13:48). The spatial aspect of the word is also used in an abstract way. Satan is portrayed as having filled the heart of Ananias (Acts 5:3). By far the most glorious application is Paul's statement in Colossians 2:9-10: 'In Christ all the fulness of the Deity lives in bodily form, and you have been given fulness in Christ.' It is not difficult to imagine a full container, but it is hard to visualize spiritual fulness. Perhaps a homely illustration would help. When we were first married we went out to lunch one day. As my bride poured her tea into the cup we continued talking, and soon her cup overflowed into the saucer. This overflowing fulness is the picture of God's supply in our lives.

A second use of our word is *fulfilment of time*. The Lord Jesus was born of the virgin, according to Galatians 4:4, 'when the time had fully come'. There is a marvellous sense of completion in that phrase. All of the sacrificial system of the Old Testament reached its climax in the Lamb of God. Prophecy likewise found its fulfilment *par excellence* in the person of Christ. In fact, there are more than thirty references to the fulfilment of prophecy in the person of Christ as the story is found in the Gospels.

Human prophecies are often unfulfilled. One remembers the boast of Adolf Hitler in 1933, that he would initiate a millennial kingdom. (Just think how unbearable a thousand years of his high-pitched harangue would have been!) In the event, Hitler's 'thousand-year reign' faded like a dead flower in 1944. The monument which is most descriptive is that mound of earth in East Berlin, scene of Hitler's bunker and burial place. True fulfilment of prophecy requires divine intervention. God must be the source, and He must fulfil it.

A third meaning of the word is closely connected; it is *finishing action.* In Romans 11:25 Paul speaks of the evangelization of the Gentiles in terms of a completed action in the future. There will come a time when 'the full number of the Gentiles has come in'. To the Thessalonians Paul also wrote of completion. God gives the success to our service, so Paul prayed 'that by His power He might fulfil every good purpose of yours and every act prompted by your faith' (2 Thessalonians 1:11). When one enrols in college there is a statement of the requirements for the course of study. Throughout the years one works steadily to achieve those standards. At the end one is qualified because one has fulfilled the requirements. God is fulfilling His sovereign plan in our world, and some day that will be completed. Then comes His glorious reign.

Fulness is an attribute of our God. He fills His world even now, because He is omnipotent. The Ephesian letter assures us that we as believers may be 'filled to the measure of all the fulness of God' (Ephesians 3:19). Therefore we sing lustily the great hymn:

Full salvation! full salvation!
Lo, the fountain opened wide!

17.
Unity of the Spirit

*'Keep the **unity** of the Spirit'* (Eph. 4:3)

Church unity is big business. There is a massive headquarters in Geneva to prove it. Dozens of committees 'keep minutes and waste hours', as the saying goes. Executive secretaries jet hither and thither coercing reluctant churches into the ecumenical fold. Doctrine is swept under the carpet by these fanatics known by some as 'ecumaniacs'.

Such institutional unity bears little resemblance to the oneness portrayed by Paul in Ephesians. He uses a relatively unknown word to describe this, the word *henotēs*. Twice does this little Greek term occur in the Ephesian letter. In Ephesians 4:3 it is described as 'unity of the Spirit through the bond of peace'. When peace prevails in the church, local and universal, unity arises. It is a spiritual unity and is not to be confused with organized uniformity.

Later in Ephesians 4 we encounter again the word 'unity'. In verse 13 it is based upon 'faith and the knowledge of the Son of God'. It issues in spiritual maturity and a full comprehension of Christ. Too often we see attempts at unity founded upon the benevolent neglect of doctrine. According to the apostle, unity arises only when we are spiritually mature and doctrinally informed. Such unity is not fostered by rhythmically clapping, shouting 'Hallelujah!' or mindless ecstasy, but rather by growing awareness of the Lord as revealed in Scripture.

Seldom have we employed ancient literature to cast light upon a biblical term. The word 'unity' can be seen at its best in the letter sent by Ignatius to the Ephesians. Writing at the end of the first century, he echoes Paul's principles concerning church unity. Ignatius urged the Ephesians to 'become a unity' (14:1). They were to 'sound together in unison' (5:1). This was apparently a reference to their testimony in the city of Ephesus. This unity, according to Ignatius, was of the same order as our unity with God. It was to be a deep unity based upon spiritual truth. Having quoted Ignatius, we have exhausted to some degree the use of this word in ancient literature. (One must bear in mind Ignatius' well-known views concerning the role of the bishop as unifier.)

Although Paul used different words for it, he taught the necessity of unity in many of his letters. The contentious Corinthians were urged by the apostle to break down divisions and foster unity (1 Corinthians 1:10). The Galatians were enjoined to be 'all one in Christ' (Galatians 3:28). To the Philippians Paul wrote commanding them to 'stand ... as one man for the faith of the gospel' (Philippians 1:27). Colossian Christians were to 'put on love, which binds them all together in perfect unity' (Colossians 3:14). The church of Jesus Christ is credible only when it stands united before a fragmented world.

The tie that binds

Almost anyone can snap a string. Very few can rip a rope in two. The principle of unity is there to be seen. Alone, we are weak and vulnerable. When we stand together with other believers we are strong. As Benjamin Franklin, the American revolutionary, said, 'We must all hang together or, most assuredly, we shall all hang separately.'

In Ephesians 4 the apostle lists seven bonds which tie Christians together and strengthen their unity. First, there is *one body* (v.4). The church is like a human body. Each member fulfils his or her function under the absolute superintendence of the Head, the Lord. We are not several unrelated groups of believers, but one organic unity. Local churches are simply manifestations of the church (Ephesians 4:15-16).

There is likewise only *one Spirit* (4:4). Every believer has been 'sealed' by one Spirit (1:13). There are no second-class Christians who limp along without the Holy Spirit's presence waiting for a sudden spiritual charge to give them energy. Every believer is sealed by the Spirit and is capable of being filled by Him repeatedly (5:18).

Believers are likewise united in looking towards *one hope* (4:4). The ultimate object of God's grace in calling us to repentance and faith is glory. Our eternal destiny with the Lord is the hope to which we have been called (1:18). By contrast, those who are without the Lord are also 'without hope and without God in the world' (2:12). As someone said, 'We believe in the eternal security of the believer and the eternal insecurity of the unbeliever.' Perhaps that is not a theologically precise statement but it makes the point. Man without God is hopeless!

There is a second triad of bases to our unity. We have *one Lord* (v.5). According to Ephesians 1:22, Jesus Christ has been given absolute sovereignty over all things. He is thus Lord of all. No single event in human history is out of God's control or awareness. Even that old fox Satan is a tame dog on a lead. He can only operate within God's set limits. Jesus Christ is Lord to the glory of God the Father. Because He is absolutely Lord He alone is Lord.

There is only *one faith* (v.5). This refers to an elementary body of biblical doctrine. All true believers adhere to the deity of Christ, His substitutionary atonement and His resurrection from the dead. Although we evangelicals shy away from reciting creeds in public worship, there is something to be said for Christians' repeating a biblical statement like the Apostle's Creed. This unity of faith is seen in missionary activity, especially in the great old missionary agencies like the Overseas Missionary Fellowship. Upon a basic biblical statement they united Christians from many confessions and countries to evangelize China (China Inland Mission). Now this great society spreads its godly influence into many countries bearing witness to one faith. It is, as Jude (v.3) stated it, 'the faith once for all entrusted to the saints'.

One baptism also unites believers. We are 'baptised by one Spirit into the body' (1 Corinthians 12:13). This initiation by the Holy Spirit and immersion in His presence and power characterizes all Christians. The concrete practice of baptism in water is also a characteristic of all true believers (Matthew 28:19).

Christians also belong to one family with *one God and Father* (v.6). In the Ephesian letter Paul makes much of the fatherhood of God. In Ephesians 1:3, He is the 'God and Father of our Lord Jesus Christ', and the emphasis here is trinitarian. He is also the source of all our spiritual knowledge (1:17), reminding us that we do not discover God by reason but by revelation. In prayer we come boldly to our loving, accessible Father (2:18). He is the Father from whom His 'whole family [fatherhood] in heaven and on earth derives its name' (3:14-15). In Ephesians 4:6 this teaching concerning the fatherhood of God reaches a climax. He is over all creatures, Sustainer of all things and pervasive in all. God the Father is sovereign.

The unity of believers is not an emotion conjured up by exciting worship or deep fellowship. The basis is the solid teaching of our God — Father, Son and Holy Spirit. As Alexander McLaren summarized it: 'The heathen have many gods because they have no one that satisfied hungry hearts ... Happy are they who turn away from the many to embrace the One.'

18.
Mature believers

'Until we all ... become **mature***'* (Eph. 4:13)

Usually one thinks of maturity in terms of physical or emotional growth. The teenage boy's voice becomes deeper; usually this happens in humorously irregular stages. A squeaky high voice is combined with manly bass. A beard sprouts in patches all over his face. Shaving is at first a treat; later it becomes a torture. To his amazement he comes to regard girls as friends rather than enemies! The longer adolescence endures, the more friendly he becomes towards girls. The lad is growing up and becoming a mature man. By the twenty-fifth birthday one can usually see the broad outlines of his manhood, his maturity.

The word used in Ephesians 4:13 is otherwise translated as 'perfect', 'finished' or 'fulfilled'. It is the Greek word *teleios*, and it is reflected in our English word 'teleology', the philosophical study of final purpose. This stream of philosophical thought holds that there is an ultimate purpose in the universe, and knowledge can only be fulfilled or complete when one considers this.

Paul used the word almost exclusively to refer to the growing-up process of believers. In Ephesians 4:13 he views the maturity of believers as being essential to a united and active church. Indeed, this maturing process is the end result of the church's ministry. As Christians learn the basics of belief they grow more effective in their service (Ephesians 4:12), more united in their fellowship (Ephesians 4:13) and more mature in their spiritual life. The symptoms of infantile behaviour fade away and they become men and women of faith. The truth implicit is profound: the church is not a crèche for crying babies but a community for responsible adult service and worship. Therefore we all reach 'unity in the faith ... knowledge of the Son of God ... and maturity, attaining to the whole measure of the fulness of Christ' (Ephesians 4:12-13).

For adults only

The word 'adult' has attracted some strange associations in modern parlance. 'Adult movies' pander to the adolescent nature of middle-aged men. 'Adult entertainment' is often riddled with language supposedly unfit for children and obviously unfit for the intelligent mind. In a typically twisted way, 'adult' becomes confused with 'childish'.

The New Testament uses our word 'mature' to describe growth in Christian understanding and behaviour. *Adult thinking* is the first use. Paul repeated this in his Corinthian letters, because of the immature characteristics of Corinthian Christianity. 'In regard to evil be infants,' he wrote, 'but in your thinking be adults' (1 Corinthians 14:20). They were to be completely uninitiated into evil practices but totally competent to think maturely. It is interesting to notice the context of this verse: it pertains to spiritual gifts. In essence the apostle asserts, 'Do not be carried away with the glittering gifts of the miraculous, but occupy yourselves with those things which edify.'

A second aspect of maturity is *adult spiritual food*. To the Hebrews the apostolic writer wrote, 'Solid food is for the mature, who by constant use have trained themselves to distinguish good from evil' (Hebrews 5:14). This principle holds true both for the preacher and his hearers. Many preachers appeal to spiritual babies by flippantly superficial sermons. (Someone called them 'sermonettes for Christian-ettes!) These are usually a good thought embroidered with a collection of stories. True solid meat is the consecutive exposition of Scripture which avoids none of the 'hard questions' and applies the Scriptures seriously to the life of individuals, families and the church. Perhaps the pathetic state of European and American Christianity is attributable to the shallow sermons being served up Sunday by Sunday.

A third use of our word is in describing the *fully taught* Christian. To the Colossians Paul wrote, 'We proclaim him [Christ], admonishing and teaching everyone with all wisdom, so that we may present everyone perfect [mature] in Christ' (Colossians 1:28). Although no one has 'arrived' spiritually (Philippians 3:13-16), we are in the process of maturing. It is this growth which must command a place of priority in every believer's life. It is amazing how much effort we expend on education. Likewise, we endeavour to train our children socially, so they can exist in polite society without reflecting adversely on us. We also give them the benefit (or plague) of music lessons, riding lessons or skating lessons. Our object is to 'give them everything we never had', whether they want it or not. Too often, however, spiritual growth is relegated to the realm of choice. Otherwise serious parents are heard to say, 'We do not want to force Christianity on them. They may rebel.' Their spiritual maturity must keep pace with their physical and mental growth, otherwise we shall have a generation of intellectual giants and spiritual pygmies. Perhaps it has already come!

Fourth, 'maturity' refers to *full development*. This is the result of all that has been said before. James found a sensitive spot when he wrote, 'If anyone is never at fault in what he says, he is a perfect [mature] man, able to keep his whole body in check' (James 3:2). Here the analogy is athletic. In Bristol we have the Olympic figure-skating champion, Robin Cousins. He began as a lad with a chance visit to the ice rink at Bournemouth. After years of relentless training he became champion of Europe and the 1980 Winter Olympics. Every movement has been studied, practised and perfected. He had trudged through the gloom and rain to the ice-skating rink every morning. Because he needed uninterrupted practice, he went at 5 or 6 o'clock in the morning. No sacrifice for Robin or his parents was too great. No pain was shunned. The target was championship, and he achieved it. This is the spiritual discipline to which the apostle James referred. When the Lord controls our behaviour we are 'mature', and this maturity is seen best in our speech. It seems that the tongue is the last faculty to capitulate to Christ's Lordship. Therefore, one whose tongue is tamed by the Saviour is described as a 'perfect [mature] man'.

Finally, we find the *pattern of maturity*. It is the Lord. During His sermon on the mount, the Lord stated this truth: 'Be perfect, therefore, as your heavenly Father is perfect' (Matthew 5:48). Certainly, the sermon on the mount was given as a standard of Christian living. Christ made the commandments internal; not outward conformity but inward attitude is our obedience to the law of God. Conditions of human weakness, poverty, hunger, persecution, etc. are hallmarks of spiritual strength, wealth, satisfaction and acceptance. In many ways our word 'mature' (or 'perfect') is a target at which we aim rather than a description of our lives. We may appear to be spiritual when compared with other Christians, but the perfection of our heavenly Father shows us up for what we are.

Lest we be discouraged by this injunction to perfection, we must cite one further text. In Hebrews 12:2 we are introduced to the Lord as 'author and perfector' of our faith. Not only are we commanded to be 'mature', we are enabled by the Lord. Therefore we 'run with perseverence the race marked out for us,' and 'fix our eyes on Jesus'.

19.
Baby believers

*'We will no longer be **infants**'* (Eph. 4:14)

Everyone loves a baby. I remember vividly the 'Baby Contest' staged by a black church in Chicago. We were assisting in the Sunday School, and the Sunday afternoon was normally given over to some social (and sadly irreverent) display. One of these homespun events was a baby-judging contest to determine the most intelligent, adorable, robust infant. The result was outrageous, but the babies were delightful.

Babies charm parents and grandparents by their smile and their gestures. Every human characteristic gains in beauty when it is reduced to baby-size. If a baby does not show normal signs of growth, however, worry soon displaces delight. The worried mum and dad dash off to the paediatrician for explanation and reassurance. When some physical or mental defect is discovered, the sorrow is deep. Slowly parents reconcile themselves to living with and caring for a 'retarded' child.

It is this problem which Paul here raises. He urges Christians at Ephesus to stop being 'infants'. The Greek word used here is *nepios*, and it refers to very young children who are not capable of eating solid food or even speaking. In Ephesians 4:14 there is a definition of spiritual infancy. Convictions are held very lightly, and every new fad sweeps them off their feet. One thinks of the little child whose 'attention span' is woefully short, and who flits from one toy to the other, never settling for long on any one plaything. Another aspect of spiritual infancy is the ease with which they are deceived. Any ingratiating speaker can draw them away from their spiritual foundations. It is like the small child who is constantly endangered by unscrupulous adults bearing sweets. How many young Christians are lured away into spiritual disaster by sweet-bearing religious quacks!

Paul urges the Ephesians to be 'no longer infants'. 'Grow up,' is his injunction to them. No exhortation is more appropriate to the spiritual crèches which pass for churches in the Western world.

Childlike not childish

Our word 'infant' has four distinct uses in the New Testament. The positive principle of 'childlike' faith and obedience is contrasted with the negative characteristic of 'childish' behaviour.

Jesus appreciated the *insight of infants*, that is, of very young children. When the children greeted Him with shouts of 'Hallelujah!' Jesus commended them by quoting Psalm 8:2: 'From the lips of children (*nepios*) and infants you have ordained praise' (Matthew 21:16-17). Children have a disarming habit of speaking candidly. One recalls the story of the pastor who asked a young mother if she would like him to read Scripture. She turned to her child and said, 'Go fetch the book which mummy loves so much.' Think of the embarrassment when the little one returned with the mail-order catalogue! 'Out of the mouth of children and infants' comes some pretty shrewd spiritual insight.

A second use of the word is also positive, *childlike faith*. Through this childlike attitude simple saints receive spiritual revelation which is often missed by the more complex mind. Jesus praised His Father for hiding His truth from 'the wise and learned' and revealing it instead to 'little children' (*nepios*). A child can accept truth from a loving parent without the destructive alloy of doubt. When I was a lad in Michigan, my father and I would shoot pheasants each autumn. I never hit anything with an air rifle or shotgun, but I did love those weeks in the woods with my dad. He had been raised in a logging camp and knew the lore of the forest. Never did I doubt his ability to lead me into and out of the woods and protect me from danger. It is this simple trust which Christ commends.

The third aspect of our word is negative. It is the *immature attitude and action*. Paul often attacks this phenomenon, which he views as a threat to both the corporate and the individual Christian life. Nowhere is his criticism more clearly seen than in the first letter to the Corinthians. In 1 Corinthians 3:1-5 Paul sketches the symptoms of spiritual infants. First, the spiritually retarded Christian is attached to the world. As A.W. Tozer wrote, 'I fear any kind of stir among Christians that does not lead to repentance and result in a sharp separation of the believer from the world.'[1] Infantile Christians are like the child walking along the railing of a bridge which spans a deep gorge. One slip and disaster results.

Another sign of spiritual immaturity is superficial tastes. In the words of Paul, 'I gave you milk, not solid food, for you were not yet ready for it' (1 Corinthians 3:2). When the preacher presents anything beyond a string of amusing anecdotes, the immature Christian mentally or even physically walks out, uttering the opinion that sermons are boring. The truth of the matter is this: he is simply too infantile to receive biblical truth. Saved he may be, but there is no indication of maturity. It is like a child who would live on Coca-Cola and crisps. Wise parents insist on feeding the child nourishing food, and wise spiritual leaders will give Christians a diet of consistent biblical exposition.

Spiritual infants express themselves in temper tantrums. According to 1 Corinthians 3:3, they are marked by 'jealousy and quarrelling'. Every pastor or church leader knows Christians who constantly attack other Christians. Never are they satisfied with the worship or work of the church. When asked to contribute to the life of the church, they are always either too busy or too upset. Criticism is the only contribution they ever are capable of making.

The inevitable result of this infantile attitude is division. Paul observed and corrected this in the Corinthian church, and he traced its cause to the childish Christians (1 Corinthians 3:4-5). By devoting an unusual amount of space to spiritual immaturity, I am attempting to show the danger of this phenomenon. No church is free of it, and the dead state of much so-called evangelicalism is directly attributable to it.

There is a fourth major aspect of this word 'infant'. It is the person who is *legally a minor*. To the Galatians Paul wrote, 'As long as the heir is a child [*nepios*], he is no different from a slave' (Galatians 4:1). Jews were legally under age until Christ came to make them sons, with all the rights and privileges pertaining to that position. Now they can call God '*Abba*, Father' (Galatians 4:6). The privileges of an heir are held by the believer. He is no longer a child but a son of God.

Although other New Testament writers used the word, it was the apostle Paul who gave it both negative and positive content. Negatively, Christians are to develop beyond infantile appetites (1 Corinthians 3:1) and speech (1 Corinthians 13:11). They are to stop eating and talking like babies. Positively they are to be childlike in their attitude towards malice (1 Corinthians 14:20) and in their faith towards the Lord.

[1] A.W. Tozer, *The Divine Conquest, p.120*

20.
Pointless pursuits

*'The **futility** of their thinking'* (Eph. 4:17)

The rat-race of sophisticated society here comes under the judgement of Paul's pen. First-century Ephesians were consumed with consumerism. Their business was tourism, catering to the religious pilgrims who worshipped at the shrine of Diana. In providing for these flocks of 'golden geese', the Ephesians spared no expense. Their city was an ancient 'Disney World' providing year-round holiday entertainment. They thought and taught that Diana had fallen from heaven, and their balance sheets confirmed this. It took the apostolic 'giant-killer' Paul, to strip away the sham.

Christians had been liberated, according to Paul, from 'the futility of their thinking' (Ephesians 4:17). The word translated 'futility' is *mataiotes,* and it means 'emptiness, futility, purposelessness and transitoriness'. The picture is one of a container which promises satisfaction, but proves to be empty.

One entire Old Testament book is devoted to the subject of 'futility'. It is, of course, Solomon's sad lament, Ecclesiastes. Opening with a general condemnation, the king wrote, 'Meaningless! Meaningless! ... Everything is meaningless' (Ecclesiastes 1:2).

The remainder of Ecclesiastes applies Solomon's sentence to most human pursuits. Pleasure is doomed to boredom. 'All things are wearisome', wrote Solomon. 'The eye never has enough of seeing, or the ear its fill of hearing' (Ecclesiastes 1:8). One thinks of the pages of pictures and print which foist upon newspaper readers every conceivable holiday activity and venue. Each one is presented as being less boring than all the others. The ultimate experience, however, ends at the unyielding wall of workday reality. John Newton was no naive youngster. He had seen the world, and he wrote,

> Fading is the worldling's pleasure,
> All his boasted pomp and show;
> Solid joys and lasting treasure
> None but Zion's children know.

Solomon then turned his scorn on aimless toil. 'There was no end to his toil ... This too is meaningless — a miserable business' (Ecclesiastes 4:8). Years ago the American singer 'Tennessee' Ernie Ford recorded a melancholy miner's song: 'You dig sixteen tons and what do you get? Another day older and deeper in debt.' Work without purpose is soul-destroying. This is as obvious to the production-line worker in a car factory, as it was to Ernie Ford's coal miner. Solomon saw this a thousand years before Christ.

Lest anyone assume that wealth brings satisfaction, Solomon also pricks that bubble. 'Whoever loves money never has enough; whoever loves wealth is never satisfied with his income. This too is meaningless' (Ecclesiastes 5:10). When I was born, my parents were recovering from the Great Depression. Money and property had proved themselves to be sand-castles swept away by the floodtide of economic disaster. In our day inflation is doing the same destructive work.

High living, too, is unmasked as a false foundation for satisfaction. Solomon, who certainly lived well, wrote, 'All man's efforts are for his mouth, yet his appetite is never satisfied ... This too is meaningless' (Ecclesiastes 6:7-9). Current studies show that modern people are preoccupied with satisfaction. Alcoholism is reaching alarming proportions, and its effect on the drinker and his or her family is documented almost daily. Even unborn children are endangered by drinking mothers, no matter how moderate their drinking. Satisfying one's appetites often brings its own reward, like the man who eats a spicy pizza pie and suffers the night through.

Solomon's conclusion is simply revolutionary: 'Remember your Creator in the days of your youth' (Ecclesiastes 12:1). More specifically, he instructs his readers to 'fear God and keep his commandments, for this is the whole duty of man' (Ecclesiastes 12:13).

Empty minds

Throughout the New Testament futility and meaninglessness are portrayed as the monopoly of the unbeliever. Life without the Lord is a guarantee for monotony and purposelessness. Biblical writers were moved by the Holy Spirit to paint this picture in particularly lurid colours.

First, *creation* was rendered futile and empty by sin (Romans 8:20). A harmonious world was given to man by God, and God proclaimed it 'very good'. When man succumbed to Satan's stealth, however, the environmental problems sprang from the ground like mushrooms. Genesis cites as examples the weeds in the garden and the pain of childbirth.

Second, *human life* likewise became void of meaning. Peter spoke of 'the empty way of life handed down from your forefathers' (1 Peter 1:18). Only the redemptive work of Christ could break the vicious circle of human existence. Just how empty this life is can be seen in such well-publicized people as Howard Hughes. After an early career as aviation pioneer and airplane producer, he spent his later years secluded from public view and numbed by a steady stream of narcotics. What an empty life Hughes's wealth bought!

Third, the New Testament speaks of futile speech. It was Peter again who pointed to those who 'mouth empty, boastful words' (2 Peter 2:18). Paul warned Titus to avoid controversies, arguments and quarrels which are 'unprofitable and useless (futile)' (Titus 3:9). Talk is cheap, and it is usually not worth the price. Put a pebble in a tin can and shake it. The din is horrible. Paul claims that empty (futile) thinking produces a similar din.

Fourth, man-made *religious forms* are likewise futile. In his masterful brief against idolatry, Paul points at generations who knew God but did not glorify Him as God. 'Their thinking became futile and their futile hearts were darkened' (Romans 1:21). James took up the same theme and sharpened it to a point. Anyone who claims to be religious but does not control his tongue 'deceives himself and his religion is worthless [futile]' (James 1:26). Modern unbelievers quickly assess the nature of Christian profession. Anyone who tries to live a lie in the name of Christianity is soon spotted as being hollow in heart and head.

Fifth, Paul speaks rhetorically of *futile faith*. If Jesus Christ were not really raised from the grave, our faith would be 'futile' (1 Corinthians 15:17). Contemporary theological scholars often look down their ecclesiastical noses at evangelicals. Why do we insist on the historicity of Adam? Why must we claim that Christ was a historical character capable of location in time and space? The resurrection is played down as an abstract statement concerning the renewed faith of early disciples. Paul sweeps this nonsense aside with one stroke of his pen. If Jesus Christ were still a mummy, then our faith would be as empty as a tomb. Faith presupposes fact. Because the Christian gospel rests on the bedrock of history and revelation, men and women have preached it, lived it and died for it.

Emptiness is the characteristic of life without Christ. Gentiles in Paul's day proved this, and so do unbelievers in our day. True meaning and purpose can come only when life has Christ as its content.

21.
Learning Christ

*'You did not come to **know** [learn] Christ that way'* (Eph. 4:20)

'Coming to know Christ' puts and keeps every Christian in the classroom. Nobody is too old to learn. The adage says, 'You cannot teach an old dog new tricks.' That may be true enough for dogs. It is surely not the case with Christians. Christians are always learning about the Lord, and their lives reflect this process of continuing education.

The word used here for learning, or 'coming to know', is the Greek verb *manthano*. It is related to the noun *mathetēs* (disciple). It is seen in our English word 'mathematics', a word used in New Testament times for 'astrologers'. The point of this little lesson in Greek is simple: every disciple is a learner. On the back of every Christian should be a big red 'L' for learner. As in driver training, the 'L' sign indicates that the bearer may make unpredictable moves and commit more mistakes than the tested driver. Christians, too, are often imperfect, but they are always learning. The trouble comes when one of them feels that he has no more to learn. Watch out for such dangerous persons!

The brief paragraph of Ephesians 4:20-24 abounds with advice for the learner. He has not learned Christ through the futility of the unconverted mind (v.20). In fact, unaided and unregenerate reason will lead to a head-on collision with the justice of God. The framework of our learning is stated as 'truth that is in Jesus' (v.21). Jesus Christ is truth personified (John 14:6), but He also has come as the primary vehicle of God's true Word (John 1:14). It is this truth which liberates man from blindness and bondage imposed by Satan on the human race. Exposure to the incarnate truth of God has a

transforming effect on man. He sheds the rags of sinful
behaviour (v.22) and dons the clothes of righteous and holy
living (v.24).

Every educational establishment is theoretically devoted
to the pursuit of truth. In reality each teacher views the world
through coloured spectacles. The Marxist sees the world in
terms of economic determinism. To the capitalist it can be
explained by free enterprise. The religious man interprets
history by reference to man's religious tendency. On the other
hand, an atheist claims that man is a puppet and fatalistic
natural law pulls the strings. Truth in essence must come
from outside the human race. The only such ambassador of
transcendent deity is Jesus Christ, 'the Word who became
flesh'. To learn this truth must be top priority for every
human being.

Live and learn

From conversion to the end of his life, the Christian must
forever be learning more about the Lord and His Word.
There is no 'school-leaving age' for the believer; he must be
continually taking in spiritual truth and ruthlessly applying it
to all of life. Our word 'learning' is found in several contexts.

First, it is applied to *learning from a teacher*. Jesus
commanded his hearers: 'Take my yoke upon you and learn
from me' (Matthew 11:29). To come under the yoke meant to
adopt the discipline imposed by a teacher. The master can
ask what he will; his disciple will instantly do it. Only in that
way can one learn from the master. In driver training the
teacher commands starts and stops. Speed and slowness are
also at his or her command. A wise learner follows the
teacher's instructions implicitly and passes the test. In the
Christian life we go when the Lord speaks and stop at His
command. Learning is doing, not only memorizing facts.

A second use of learning is *discovery*. To the amazement and
confusion of Paul's guards, they 'learned that he is a Roman
citizen' (Acts 23:27). In the event this produced more
respectful treatment for the apostle. Such a discovery is

sometimes negative, as it was for the Galatians. Paul probed to discover (learn) who had led them into legalism (Galatians 3:2). In the Christian life we make both positive and negative discoveries. We discover new truth from the Word and apply it to our benefit. Sometimes we also discover teachings which are diversions from the truth and lead us into rough paths. A person may discover the secret of a marvellous Christmas gift and secretly rejoice in this good gift. Another may discover the secret that he has a terminal disease and carry this load with him to the grave. Certainly the Christian should seek to discover biblical truth which will enrich his spiritual life.

Third, to learn speaks of *appropriating* truth. To Titus Paul wrote, ' Our people must learn to devote themselves to doing what is good' (Titus 3:14). We learn by doing. To master masses of religious teaching and use it as a weapon to beat the weak is neither profitable for us nor helpful for the church. Christian truth is only helpful when worked out in the life. For several years I 'learned' Spanish at school. The teacher would have said she 'taught' me Spanish. At the end my ability did not extend beyond 'Adios' and 'Gracias'. Years later we moved to Germany and started to study German. Learning became intensely practical, inasmuch as we could only purchase food through the vehicle of the German language. Furthermore, our ministry depended solely upon our ability to communicate in German. It was amazing how much faster we mastered German. This practical learning is exactly the quality of learning involved in the Christian life. It is not what we know that counts, but what we do.

Fourth, learning also refers to *hearing*. When the new song will be sung in heaven, only the redeemed will be able to hear and learn it (Revelation 14:3). One requires ears attuned to pick up spiritual truth. It is much like a radio. When the wavelengths were changed in England we discovered that our favourite programme was no longer obtainable on our little transistor set. It required a new set designed to receive 'long wave'. In the same way an unbeliever finds spiritual truth to be uninteresting, boring and incomprehensible. To read the Bible is a torture akin to the medieval wheel.

Listening to a sermon is a sure cure for insomnia. When he is born again, however, he finds the Bible has come alive. The preaching of the Word seems to be directed at him and suited to his personal needs. He has an ear attuned to hear and learn divine truth.

Learning in the Bible is not a matter of piling up facts in one's memory. Neither is it conformity to the creed of any specific church. Learning in biblical terms is the transferring of truth into practice. A true Christian is one who heeds James's injunction: 'Do not merely listen to the word, and so deceive yourselves. Do what it says' (James 1:22).

22.
Falsehood rejected

*'Put off **falsehood** and speak truthfully'* (Eph. 4:25)

'True and false' tests were quite the vogue a few years ago. A long list of statements was presented. Next to each were the letters 'T' and 'F'. If the statement corresponded with the facts dispensed by the teacher, one would mark 'T' ('true'). If the statement varied ever so slightly from the teacher's opinions the student would mark 'F' ('false'). In all cases the arbiter of truth or falsehood was the teacher, and the marking proved this.

In this little verse we have God's 'true and false' test. Christians are urged, indeed commanded, to do away with all falsehood. The word used here is *pseudos*. It often appears in English combinations. Most common of these is probably 'pseudonym', a fictitious name given to a literary character. For instance, the real name of Mark Twain, the American humorist, was Samuel Clemens. The same is true in the entertainment world. Very few people would instantly recognize the name, Marion Morrison. On the other hand, everyone knows John Wayne. A more glamorous name often lends lustre to one's public image.

Paul here is not warning of the relatively innocent embellishment of names. He is concerned with deceit within the church of Jesus Christ. In verse 31 he also rules out any 'slander', the attribution of untruth to another's character. In fact, the word here translated 'slander' is really 'blasphemy'. Just as the name of our God can be blackened by blasphemy, so can the name of a Christian brother or sister. All kinds of 'falsehood' are condemned by the apostle, and Christians are to be divorced absolutely from them.

The basic word *pseudos* (falsehood) occurs rather infrequently in the New Testament. In Romans 1:25 it is the rebellious and depraved man who 'exchanged the truth of God for a lie'. By making a false god he has robbed the true God of His rightful place and position. Paul warned the Thessalonians that Satan would produce miracles, signs and wonders, but all these would be 'falsehood', a lie (2 Thessalonians 2:9). In the summing up of the divine Judge found in Revelation 21 very little is left to one's imagination. Certainly that which is 'deceitful' (false) is condemned and excluded from God's glorious heaven (Revelation 21:27).

Having briefly sketched the pedigree of our word 'falsehood', we must also see the context in which Paul used it. He is not addressing the unbeliever but rather the church of Jesus Christ at Ephesus. They are to 'put off falsehood'. Surely we, too, stand in need of such exhortation. We must put off falsehood in terms of our communication with one another. Let no Christian utter sweet, sentimental words to a fellow Christian and then slay him with words when he is out of earshot. Let no Christian sing lustily the songs of heaven on Sunday and revert to the 'earthy' language of the gutter on Monday. Neither dare a child of God mouth the right words in worship and converse familiarly about the things of God and then behave just like the modern pagans with whom he engages in daily business.

Do not be a 'pseudo-Christian'! Instead put off falsehood and allow the truth of God to penetrate into every compartment of your life. Nothing is secular to the saint, every aspect of life must be brought within the realm of God's truthfulness.

True and false

A man is known by the company he keeps. So are words. This word, 'falsehood', keeps pretty grim company. In the New Testament it is almost always used in conjunction with another term. Predictably these compound titles are all negative.

Paul warned the Galatian Christians about *false brothers.*
These could be expected to 'infiltrate our ranks to spy on the
freedom we have in Christ Jesus and to make us slaves'
(Galatians 2:4). I recall the story told by a courageous old
brother in Berlin. During the war Gestapo agents would slip
into the services to spy on saints. These 'false brothers' were
unmasked by a simple method. No hymn-books were passed
out, and the Gestapo agents were soon revealed by their
ignorance of the hymns.

A second and more dangerous brand of fakes is the *false
apostle.* Paul branded them as 'deceitful workmen', masquer-
ading as apostles of Christ' (2 Corinthians 11:13). Recently
we were late in leaving for church. The doorbell rang, and
two rather pleasant ladies stood waiting. They explained that
they were witnesses to Jehovah. Their zeal was apostolic;
their message was satanic.

Third, there were many *false teachers* preying upon first-
century churches. Peter warned of them because they would
'secretly introduce destructive heresies, even denying the
sovereign Lord who bought them' (2 Peter 2:1). The apostle
John was likewise at pains to warn believers. He called them
'false prophets' and condemned their teaching, which denied
the incarnation of the Lord Jesus Christ (1 John 4:1-3).
Christians were to resist this devious doctrine with all their
strength. Such falsifiers should not even gain entrance into a
Christian home (2 John 10). Deception is rendered more
dangerous today by the religious appearance of many
deceivers. Professors of theology deny the inspiration of
Scripture. Bishops decry Christian standards as being archaic
and Victorian. World religious leaders urge us to seek
redemptive features in non-Christian religions. The evangelist
is accused of 'proselytizing'.

Fourth, the Scriptures make frequent reference to *false
witnesses.* From the Lord's time onwards this devilish device
has been employed to discredit true disciples. At the trial of
Jesus the religious leaders 'were looking for false evidence
against Jesus so they could put him to death. But they did not
find any, though many witnesses came forward' (Matthew

26:59-60). When Stephen was stoned, too, evidence was presented by false witnesses (Acts 6:13). Today those who seek to suppress true Christianity also use this time-tested instrument. In his fascinating autobiography, *Three Generations of Suffering*, the embattled Russian Baptist, Georgi Vins, wrote, 'My mother was placed in Lukyanov prison in Kiev. The fabrication of a criminal case began ... How all of this brings to mind the years 1930 to 1937, when a criminal case was made out three times against my father.' 'If the world hates you,' Jesus taught, 'keep in mind that it hated me first ... You do not belong to the world ... That is why the world hates you' (John 15:18-19).

Finally, the Scriptures speak of *false Christs.* 'For false Christs and false prophets will appear and perform great signs and miracles to deceive even the elect — if that were possible' said the Lord concerning the last days (Matthew 24:24). Certainly the world has been visited by such 'pseudo-messiahs'. During the previous century Karl Marx appeared proclaiming materialistic redemption to the proletariat. In our age Adolf Hitler emerged as the saviour of Germany, only to become the destroyer of Western Europe. In the religious sphere, one thinks of a Sun Myung Moon, who declares himself to be the finisher of Christ's earthly work. False Christs abound, but the real One has yet to make His return appearance. Nevertheless, 'the Lord is not slow in keeping His promise, as some understand slowness. He is patient with you, not wanting anyone to perish, but everyone to come to repentance' (2 Peter 3:9). He will come and show up for ever all the false Christs.

23.
God's mimics

'Be **imitators** of God' (Eph. 5:1)

An English student of the famous Marcel Marceau was interviewed on the B.B.C. She told how students were taught all day by the famous French mimic; each evening they watched him perform. When they returned to their native lands, they bore the indelible mark of the master.

This is the picture which Paul employs in Ephesians 5:1. We are to be 'imitators' or 'mimics' of God. The Greek word *mimetai* lies at the root of such English derivatives as 'mimic', 'mime', 'panto*mime*' (all imitating), 'mimeograph' (duplicating machine), etc. In each case the basic thought is 'copying exactly'. The 'mimic' seeks to portray a person or animal in such a way that the audience is left in no doubt as to the subject depicted. 'Pantomimes' were plays without words; the actors sought to tell a story by imitation. In America the duplicating machine is called a 'mimeograph', because it more or less faithfully reproduces hundreds of copies of an original skin.

The apostle urged upon Ephesian Christians the necessity of imitating God. Another picture is used to underline his injunction, because Christians are to act like 'dearly loved children' of God. Children are natural mimics, and one sees this repeatedly. When we went to Germany our daughter was not quite two years old. She rapidly learned the difficult German language and duplicated, 'mimicked' sounds which we learned only with great difficulty and after prolonged study. Children also mime the actions of their parents. A little one crawls into the driver's seat of a car and tries to drive like daddy. (I tried this at age three, and ended up in a ditch across

the road from my grandparents' home.) Meanwhile a little
girl loves to cook and bake like her mum, even though the
cakes may be mud and the tea imaginary.

Christians are to imitate God with special regard to love.
As He loves us and sacrificed His only Son on our behalf, so
we are to show sacrificial love. Psychologists tell us that a
person can only show love, if he or she has been shown love.
Since God demonstrated His love to us in the offering of the
Lord Jesus Christ, we can also make sacrifices in showing our
love. We also learn something of the essence of love. Love is
not only pretty words and super-sentimental songs. Love is
acting in a sacrificial manner towards someone else. So
Christians are to imitate God by loving others. No cost is too
great to be paid, and we must be everlastingly at it. One
wonders if the gospel would not be more credible to outsiders,
were the love of Christians more visibly sacrificial.

Whom do you imitate?

When I left college, Billy Graham was the foremost American
preacher. His distinctive high-speed delivery and his
evangelistic addresses were copied by many young preachers
in the late fifties. Close your eyes in any Youth for Christ
Rally across America, and you would think that Billy
Graham was reincarnated in a hundred different towns and
cities on any given Saturday night. (Actually, preaching is
probably best learned by imitation, and we could use a few
Spurgeons and Martyn Lloyd-Joneses in Britain today.)

Paul makes much of learning by imitation. He urges
Christians in the first instance to *copy himself*. To the
schismatic saints at Corinth, Paul wrote, 'Follow my
example, as I follow the example of Christ' (1 Corinthians
11:1). He made the same statement to Thessalonian
Christians: 'For you yourselves know how you ought to follow
our example' (2 Thessalonians 3:7). Just as a coach
demonstrates the movements required of a footballer and
then makes the lad copy them, so a Christian follows the
pattern of mature believers.

Another aspect of this imitation is seen in the Thessalonian letters. To those who had recently abandoned paganism for Christ, Paul said, 'You, brothers, became *imitators of God's churches* in Judea' (1 Thessalonians 2:14). The context reveals that they were imitating the suffering of fellow Christians. From Eastern Europe and other totalitarian states come reports of Christians suffering. When one local congregation suffers, another is encouraged to follow suit. Like suffering, evangelism and missionary activity are also learned by imitation. The church in which I grew up in America planted seven small churches in outlying neighbourhoods. These grew into strong independent fellowships which today vie for size with the parent church. Each one of them imitated the original in a strong Sunday School ministry and a sacrificial missionary programme.

Paul's ultimate command is *imitation of the Lord*. Again the Thessalonians were the recipients of this commendation: 'You became imitators of us and of the Lord' (1 Thessalonians 1:6). This sounds blatantly presumptuous. How can a human being in any way imitate the infinite God? The early Christians seemed to emulate Christ's life-style. They were very cautious of materialism; the Lord did not even own His own home. They were thoroughly committed to help others. Their Lord had gone about doing good (Acts 10:38), until His very goodness became a source of offence. The Lord had helped the sick and sinful, and the disciples emulated this individually and collectively as a church. Their imitation of the Lord led them to a totally sacrificial life-style which stood out in bold contrast with the acquisitive society of the ancient world. One wonders whether the church in Europe and America does not imitate the world more than the Lord. With an increasing emphasis on wealth, management procedures, the multiplication of committees and the use of secular publicity, we have become almost indistinguishable from scores of charitable secular societies. The only difference is their greater commitment to benevolent ends.

The apostles not only told Christians whom they should imitate, the New Testament also gave detailed instructions on what Christians should imitate. John instructed Christians not to imitate what is evil but *'what is good'* (3 John 11). From the time of Machiavelli (1469-1527) onwards the principle has been repeatedly illustrated: 'Might is right.' One sees this in the burgeoning trade union movement or the dominance of the boardroom over weaker workmen. Racial minorities in many countries have capitalized on their numerical strength to impose their will on the populace. In some parts of America, even a homosexual minority can turn an election to its advantage. Ethical standards seem to fade before naked power. Christians on the other hand must consider God's standards of right and regulate all behaviour according to that guideline.

A second worthy object of imitation is *faith*. Predictably the author of Hebrews urged Christians: 'Remember your leaders, who spoke the Word of God to you. Consider the outcome of their way of life and imitate their faith' (Hebrews 13:7). We are constantly reminded of Hudson Taylor. With reliance on nothing but faith he led a group of 641 missionaries in China.

A final imitable characteristic is *patience*. It is related in essence to faith, and the writer of Hebrews links them in Hebrews 6:12: 'Imitate those who through faith and patience inherit what has been promised.' Patience is in short supply. In fact, perhaps patience is running out at a faster rate than oil. Christians have been impatient for so long that they have convinced themselves impatience is a virtue. It is transmuted into urgency: 'The Lord's work requireth haste' is perversely misquoted to justify their impatience. One recalls the incident in rush-hour traffic. A woman tried in vain to start her car at the traffic lights. Meanwhile a harassed businessman hammered his horn. Finally the woman got out and walked slowly back to her fellow motorist. 'Perhaps you would like to attempt starting my car,' she enquired, 'then I could lean on the horn for you.' Faith and patience are twin virtues, according to Hebrews. Both are learned by imitation.

Early disciples of the Lord were called 'Christians' (Acts 11:26). This was a term of derision designed to destroy their confidence and their growing influence. Instead, the 'little Christs' turned the nickname into a badge of honour, one which true believers still bear with dignity.

24.
Shining lights

*'Now you are **light** in the Lord'* (Eph. 5:8)

When I was a lad we often sang a chorus:

This little light of mine
I'm going to let it shine.

It was a simple little ditty, but its truth was profound. God calls us out of the gloom to make us true lights, luminaries in a dark world. Ephesians, along with other New Testament writings, contains some enlightening words about this subject.

The Greek word used here is *phos*. We see it in many English words. 'Phosphorous' is a combination of two Greek words meaning 'light-bearing', and it refers in English to a substance which glows in the dark. A 'photoelectric' cell is a device which is triggered into action by light. Perhaps the most common use is 'photograph', where an image is imprinted ('written') on paper made sensitive to light.

Just as there are many English uses of *phos* and *photo* (another form of the word), so the Bible is resplendent with references. Ephesians 5:8-14 is an example *par excellence*. The Lord is the light source, according to Ephesians 5:8. Just as light requires connection to the mains or some source of power, so the Christian must be connected to the divine Power Source, the Lord Jesus Christ.

Once associated by faith with Christ, Christians become 'light in the Lord' and 'children of light' (Ephesians 5:8). The principle which applies here is reflection. As the moon reflects sunlight, so Christians reflect the 'Son-light'. They are luminous forces in our morally and spiritually darkened world, because they transmit to it the light of the Lord. It is all picture language, but the common use of light makes this picture easily comprehensible.

The 'fruit of the light' is seen in a different quality of life. The 'children of light' are marked by *goodness*. This is a moral and spiritual excellence which consistently pursues the best advantage of others. Self is seriously and ruthlessly subjected to the good of other people. A second characteristic of these light-bearers is *righteousness*. Here the emphasis falls on following the line without diversion. A Christian adheres to God's guidelines without veering off. In these days of darkly deviant behaviour, Christians stand out as bright spots. Finally, the 'children of light' are committed to the *truth*. They are marked by genuineness which stands out against the prevailing background of deception and hypocrisy. There may be hypocrites inside and outside of churches, but there is no room for them in the church of the Lord Jesus Christ (Ephesians 5:9).

The final aspect of this light is exposure. Light exposes sin (Ephesians 5:13). The penetrating effect of light is seen in this verse. An X-ray penetrates the flesh and reveals broken bones and spotted lungs, and God's light pierces through to the heart of man. It reveals all the sin-scars inside and it also shows up the fractures in man-made righteousness. Light also heals. Much eye surgery is now performed by light, the super-ray of a laser beam. Thus God exposes and heals man's mortal sinfulness by the light of His person and Word.

Lighting up the world

Light is so basic to our existence that it appears repeatedly throughout the Bible. In fact, the first creative act of God was light (Genesis 1:3). Without light we should have been like a race of blind rodents. Light provides warmth and illumination, but it also gives growth to the plants we eat. Therefore without it we should have been deprived of life itself.

God is characterized by light. He is the One who dwells in light (1 Timothy 6:16). He has no need of sleep or night, so light is an everlasting element of God's existence. From that realm of light He sent into our world the Light, the Lord Jesus Christ. John 1:1-9 portrays Christ as the Light which lights every man who comes into the world. A.W. Tozer wrote of this: 'In the hearts of all men the light shines, the word sounds, and there's no escaping them.' He is the Light of the world, according to His own teaching (John 8:12). All other light creatures are pale reflections of Him and His presence in heaven will preclude them all (Revelation 21:23).

The second use of light pertains to *spiritual enlightenment*. At the end of the eighteenth century a philosophical movement was born which embraced almost every academic discipline and finally spilled over into common use. It was called 'The Enlightenment'. In his famous definition of 'Enlightenment', Immanuel Kant said it was an emancipation proclamation. Man was emancipated from God's control and enabled to use reason as his sole guide to right and wrong. Latter-day philosophers such as Jean-Paul Sartre have applied this principle to successive generations. The Bible, however, portrays human wisdom as being flawed. Man will always run up against barriers, when he relies solely on his wit. God has given man a divine source of light, however, which shows him the way to regulate his life. John the apostle wrote, 'The darkness is passing and the true light is already shining' (1 John 2:8).

Because the true light has appeared, there has sprung up a spiritual generation of *'children of light'*. Their lives have been subjected to the scrutiny of the light, and this light has revealed their sinfulness. God has not only shown their sin, He has also single-handedly forgiven and cleansed it. This introduces into human society an entirely new element. Now Christians go out as 'lights in the world' (Matthew 5:14, 16). Wherever they go, they convey this light and the light of their lives rebukes the world and its sin. They are comparable to natural light in every way. They give illumination of the world's situation. Through them the world can see its sad state. They also give healing just as a laser beam performs delicate surgery. They are a healing force in a fatally ill world.

The wise king Solomon had it right when he wrote, 'The path of the righteous is like the first gleam of dawn, shining ever brighter till the full light of day.'

25.
Spirit filled

*'Be **filled** with the Spirit'* (Eph. 5:18)

Blow into a child's balloon, and the air penetrates to every part. Soon it is round and large, and it becomes a source of delight to the child. (When it bursts, of course, it may bring more distress than delight to the adults!) The balloon is useless until it has been blown up; it is just a flabby rubber disc.

Christians, too, are only spiritually successful when they are filled with the Spirit. The word translated 'Spirit' is *pneuma* in Greek. We see it in such English relatives as 'pneumatic', a machine operated by air pressure. 'Pneumonia' is a disease affecting the lungs and hindering the breathing. This connection between the 'Spirit' and 'air' was also known to the Greeks. It is seen in the Lord's word play: 'The wind blows wherever it pleases... So it is with everyone born of the Spirit' (John 3:8).

Being filled with the Spirit is the privilege of every Christian, and the apostle gives some basic teaching in Ephesians 5:18. First, being filled with the Spirit is stated in command form. It is the responsibility of believers. One cannot simply sit back and wait for it to happen; being filled with the Spirit depends on the direct decision of believers. Just as eating is not automatic, so being filled with the Spirit requires the exertion of spiritual effort.

Second, the command to be filled with the Spirit is stated in the plural. An American idiom might express this more clearly: ' "You all" be filled with the Spirit.' Spirit fulness is not the prerogative of supersaints but the responsibility of all Christians. The Christian church can only adequately fulfil its function in the world when every member knows this Spirit fulness.

Third, the command is stated in the passive voice. As the New English Bible translates this, it becomes clear: 'Let the Holy Spirit fill you.' It is similar to a container plunged into water. The container must *do* nothing except be empty. The water will rush in as a matter of course.

Finally, this verse is couched in the present tense: 'Be continually filled with the Spirit.' Continual, progressive action is characteristic of the present tense in the Greek language. Being filled with the Spirit is not a single event at a specific time in the Christian's life. It is the recurring joy of every Christian. In Bristol we have a major firm producing hot-air balloons. When the balloon is in flight it is repeatedly filled with hot air by a piece of onboard equipment. Christians are only kept aloft spiritually by the continuing fulness of the Spirit.

Having stated the principle positively, one must also make two negative statements. 'Filling' with the Spirit is not the same as being sealed with the Spirit. The Ephesian Christians were already 'sealed' with the Spirit (Ephesians 1:13). Nevertheless they were capable of grieving the Spirit (Ephesians 4:30). They required the fulness of the Spirit.

Second, this filling is also not synonymous with Spirit baptism. Corinthian Christians were baptized with the Holy Spirit (1 Corinthians 12:13). The schismatic tendencies of the Corinthian church revealed with obvious clarity that they were not filled with the Spirit. Instead they were very worldly Christians indeed (1 Corinthians 3:1-3).

The fulness of the Spirit is not a one-time, automatic Christian experience to be grasped by faith. It is a progressive, daily responsibility of all believers to be seen in their behaviour. If you are filled with the Spirit, you know it. So does everyone else.

What makes you tick?

When I learned to drive we were living in Michigan, one of the northern states in the United States. Since it was close to the Canadian border, the winters were almost arctic. One soon learned that a car battery sometimes went flat under the added strain of frigid morning starts. The only secret seemed to be a 'jump start'. When my dead battery was connected to a strong one, the tired engine sprang to life. In a real sense, the Holy Spirit gives a 'jump start' to the Christian.

This spiritual supercharge is seen in several aspects of the Christian life and exemplified best in the early church. The book of Acts is, according to some scholars, falsely titled. It should be 'The Acts of the Holy Spirit', and this is borne out in the entire scope of the story.

First, the fulness of the Holy Spirit brings *power to witness*. The Lord before His ascension promised the Holy Spirit as a source of energy for His witnesses (Acts 1:8). That this worked is seen in the subsequent performance of the disciples. Of the Jerusalem church it was said: 'After they prayed, the place where they were meeting was shaken. And they were all filled with the Holy Spirit and spoke the word of God boldly' (Acts 4:31).

This remarkable energy for witness is seen today. I remember a property broker in Manchester who for years regularly witnessed door-to-door on his executive housing estate. On the other end of the cultural scale was a military policeman who witnessed to high-ranking officers after he was converted in Berlin.

Second, the Holy Spirit's fulness gives *power to suffer*. Of Stephen, the second Christian martyr (John the Baptist was the first to die for Christ), the beloved physician Luke wrote, 'Stephen, full of the Holy Spirit, looked up to heaven and saw the glory of God, and Jesus standing at the right hand of God ... They all rushed at him, dragged him out of the city and began to stone him' (Acts 7:55-58).

Solzhenitsyn in his *Gulag Archipelago* told of 'many courageous priests who have already paid for their preaching with the blood of martyrdom'. Georgi Vins, who recently was exiled to the West, reports that this suffering is continuing.

The Holy Spirit gives grace to the suffering saint. He does not give this grace, however, until it is required. When a missionary's son was killed in an accident in France, the grieving mother said, 'I never thought I could bear this. But now God is giving me all the strength I need.'

A third evidence of the Holy Spirit's fulness is *faith*. It was said of Barnabas: 'He was a good man, full of the Holy Spirit and faith' (Acts 11:24). Only the Holy Spirit can lift one's faith from the plane of the normal to triumphant heights.

During my college years in America I heard first of 'Send the Light'. Each Christmas and Easter they took lorry loads of students to Mexico, where they sold Christian literature. The leader of that movement was George Verwer. Since then we have seen Operation Mobilization emerge and expand to include thousands of young people and two evangelistic ships, *Logos* and *Doulos*. This massive enterprise of evangelism is a trophy to the faith of George Verwer and his colleagues.

There is one final evidence of spiritual fulness, *joy*. When the gospel touched pagans in Asia Minor many were converted. This spread of salvation was an encouragement to the disciples, who were 'filled with joy and with the Holy Spirit' (Acts 13:52).

The Holy Spirit should bring joy into the Christian's life, as the sun permeates the dark corners of a room. Wherever this joy goes it gives light and warmth. No matter how a Christian suffers, he can know the Spirit's joy. I think of a dear saint at Bristol who has been crippled for many years, and the disability is increasing as I write. Still the joy of the Lord fills her life and brightens the life of everyone who visits her humble room.

Being filled with the Spirit is not reserved for the supersaints. It is the prerogative of every believer, and the Holy Spirit will fill any life which is free of known sin. The results are power to witness, faith to trust God for great things, strength to suffer and joy independent of the circumstances.

26.
Spiritual submission

'Submit *to one another out of reverence for Christ'*
(Eph. 5:21)

'Submission' conjures up ghastly images of defeat. One thinks
of the burly, sweating wrestlers on television. One whirls the
other around and pounces on him. The result is a
'submission'. This is hardly a picture calculated to deepen
devotion. It brings up all sorts of violent reaction in the
normal, civilized citizen of any land.

'Submission' in the New Testament is usually a translation
of the Greek word *hypotasso*. Actually, both parts of the word
are reflected in English. *Hypo* means 'under', and is seen in
'hypodermic' (under the skin). *Tasso* is the root from which
'tactic' comes. The root meaning of *tasso* is 'order', to put in a
line. Thus 'tactics' are the orderly plans for carrying out a
battle or any sort of a campaign. Taken together, *hypotasso*
means to order oneself under something or someone.
Spiritually, we are to be submissive to the Lord, and to each
other.

First, Paul portrays Christ as the Head of His church. All
things are in submission to Him, and He is 'head over
everything for the church' (Ephesians 1:22). The primary
premise of submission is headship. There must be someone
worthy of our submission. He is Christ alone. This is a
submission rooted in created order. Whether we acknowledge
Him or not, He is Lord. Salvation ultimately depends on
whether or not we recognize Him as Lord in time and space.
All will see His Lordship in eternity, but for the vast majority
of our race this will come too late.

A second appearance of 'submit' is in Ephesians 5:21:
'Submit one to another out of reverence for Christ.' The church

of Jesus Christ is not a herd of wild horses fighting for supremacy and running only reluctantly in a restless unity based on survival. The church resembles more closely the handsome horses who draw the royal coach on special occasions. They are matched by selection; Christians are chosen by God. They are trained to pull together; Christians are taught by the Spirit through the Word to work in unison. They are matched according to natural gifts; Christians possess spiritual gifts which determine their role in the fellowship. Therefore there can be submission to the One in the driving seat; Christ is in sovereign control over His church. Our unity results from our submission to the Lord.

In the English Bible there is another appearance of 'submission': 'Wives, submit to your husbands as to the Lord' (Ephesians 5:22). The word 'submit' does not occur in the Greek text. The proper translation would be thus: 'Submit to one another out of reverence for Christ. Wives, this is your attitude especially towards your husbands' (Ephesians 5:21-22).

There is a final appearance of 'submission' in Ephesians. In Ephesians 5:24, Paul asserts that the church 'submits' to Christ. Is this wild idealism? No! It is reality. Throughout the world and during all ages there have been faithful churches which have 'submitted' to the Lord. These were seldom in the mainstream of approved Christianity. Often they were a persecuted minority, and sometimes the opposition came from the official church itself. E.H. Broadbent's useful, though selective, *The Pilgrim Church* pursues this theme in a helpful way. May God grant that we shall be marked by submission to the living Lord of the church.

Orderly Christian society

The secret of order in society is submission. When anarchy reigns no one is safe. Not only are traditional values swept away, but with them go the freedoms guarded so jealously by our fathers. 'Submission' is not an agent of cultural, political and social repression. It is the key to survival in the present and future.

First, the Scriptures urge submission to *people and institutions.* Jesus taught by example the need of submitting to *parents.* His superior knowledge and ability did not exempt Him from such submission (Luke 2:51). Employees, most of whom were slaves in the first century, were likewise admonished to show submission towards their *employers* (Titus 2:9). On a national scale, the New Testament uniformly urges submission to the *government* of the day, even the pagan and oppressive government of the Roman empire (Romans 13:1). The late director of the Federal Bureau of Investigation, J. Edgar Hoover, drew all of these together in one statement: 'A child who has been taught to respect the laws of God will have little difficulty respecting the laws of men.'

Second, there is the requirement for submission to the *will of God.* The primary thrust of God's will concerning man is to make man righteous, right with God. This is brought into bold relief in Romans, where the necessity of 'submitting to God's righteousness' is shown as the exclusive way to peace with God (Romans 10:3). God's will for man's salvation and spiritual prosperity is not to be misunderstood. It is not fatalism, akin to the Islamic concept of *kismet.* Neither is it like the popular, romantic view expressed in Doris Day's melodic though misleading, '*Que será será,* whatever will be, will be.' Man is not a pawn on a cosmic chessboard, with mechanistic forces moving the pieces. God is in control!

Third, biblical submission is *voluntary and loving.* Paul called Corinthian Christians to be submissive (1 Corinthians 16:16). Young men in the church are to be spiritually submissive to older, more experienced and presumably mature brethren (1 Peter 5:5). Although the basic premise of Christianity is submission, it is the Spirit who makes us more submissive every day. We are not involved in a sort of religious 'shot-gun wedding'. In the old days when a father felt his daughter had been violated, he forced the lad involved to 'do the right thing by his daughter'. At the point of a shot-gun the couple were escorted to the altar. The resultant marriage can be imagined. God does not 'shot-gun' us into submission, but His Spirit softens us day by day. People call this a mellowing process; we know it is a supernatural activity of the Holy Spirit.

Fourth, the Lord told His men that even the *demons were submissive*. When they came back from their first missionary foray into enemy territory, the disciples had learned that demonic powers were intimidated in the Lord's name (Luke 10:17, 20). The Lord reminded them that the salvation of souls was infinitely more important than the public defeat of demons. We still see satanic forces bowed down beneath His feet. When we were missionaries in Germany, we saw several freed from satanic oppression and depression through the victorious name of the Lord Jesus Christ. One thinks especially of a retired man who had been consigned to Satan in payment for his healing from a childhood disease.

Submission is a recurring theme in Scripture, but it is always based upon submission to the Lord. Christians are now in submission to Him, and their lives are thus marked by His Lordship. This fact is sometimes clouded by the human weakness of individual believers. Some day, however, the glory of this submission will be seen in all its perfection. Then we shall see the fulfilment of 1 Corinthians 15:27, where Paul speaks of everything having been 'put under his feet'. Then submission will mean identification with His glory.

27.
He is Head

*'Christ is the **head** of the church'* (Eph. 5:23)

One of Paul's favourite images identifies the church with Christ's body. He is the Head of that body. As such, He is obviously indispensable, for a church which has 'lost its head' is dead.

The Greek word used here is *kephalē*, and it is related to the English word 'cephalic' (pertaining to the head). A 'brachycephalic' person has a small brain capacity, and a 'dolichocephalic' individual has a larger head. 'Hydrocephalic' children are afflicted with water on the brain;, they are seriously inhibited.

Paul used *kephalē* to describe the Lord. He is the Head of His church. In Ephesians 1:22 He is described as being 'head over everything for the church'. Because the Lord is Lord over the entire world, He is the legitimate Lord of His church.

All members of the church are related to the Lord, and they derive their strength and stimulus to action from Him. It is the aim of the church to grow together in connection with the Lord. Relationship to one another in the Christian church is based upon our relationship to the Lord. Because we are subservient to the Head, we are also submissive to and responsive to one another (Ephesians 4:15).

In Ephesians 5:23 there is a chain of authority. The wife is submissive to her husband, because the husband is submissive to the Lord. The Lord is head over His whole church. It is this all-pervading principle of submission which runs throughout the Body of Christ.

The headship of Christ teaches a negative principle also. Independence of the Lord as Head of His church is a prescription for spiritual disaster. This is stated in Colossians 2:19, where Paul asserts that he who 'has lost connection with the Head' is arrogantly unspiritual.

It is like a limb which becomes paralysed. The nerves connecting it to the brain are damaged, and the limb is no longer responsive. A leg refuses to bear weight or propel the body forward. An arm refuses to feed the mouth, and the hand rebels at the thought of writing. When any limb ceases to perform its normal function, the person is seriously ill. Likewise any Christian who is not obedient to the divine Head of the church is in serious trouble.

The true Headmaster

In England we often use the term 'headmaster' or simply 'the head'. Every school is presided over by a man or woman as 'the head'. Nothing so made a child quake in bygone days as 'the head' wielding a cane. Most teachers try to please the headmaster or headmistress too. The New Testament portrays Christ as the 'Head Master' of the church.

Predictably, the word 'head' is used in various contexts throughout the Bible. First, it is used for the *human head*. God's care is expressed by the statement of the Lord that 'the very hairs of your head are ... numbered' (Matthew 10:30). Rest is described as laying down one's head (Matthew 8:20), a phrase visible in our modern jargon: 'Get your head down.' In an abstract sense, responsibility is stated in the remark: 'Your blood be on your own heads' (Acts 18:6). When a person shows kindness to his enemy he can shame his enemy, and thus 'heap burning coals on his head' (Romans 12:20). In either its concrete or abstract form, the head is the centre of responsibility and activity. The wives of Henry VIII proved how impossible was life without a head.

Second, the most obvious use in the New Testament is describing Christ as *Head of the church*. Most churches today look to some human head. Since the Reformation the titular head of the Anglican church has been the monarch. He or she may or may not be a sincere believer, and both sorts have reigned since the Reformation. Still the crowned head is the head of the Church of England. The Roman church views the pope as its earthly head. Local churches may be led by a pastor or an elder, which position of leadership is often a subject for debate and competition. The Bible states clearly, however, 'He is the head of the body, the church' (Colossians 1:18).

Third, the husband is *head of the home*. In 1 Corinthians 11:3, we find God's economy of things. God is the Head of Christ, Christ rules over the man, and the man is the head of the home. If this chain of leadership breaks down at any point, God's plan is not fulfilled. Because of the essential unity between Christ and His Father, there was no dissension in the Godhead. Man is not always responsive to God's rule. This is disobedience which courts spiritual, social and personal disaster. By the same token, the husband must take leadership in the home. If he does not set the spiritual tone of the family, the offspring usually 'spring' away from the things of God. If he does not give love to the family, the emotional scene resembles a dry and rather dusty desert. The principle of headship runs throughout God's created order, and when it is violated there is sin.

Fourth, Christ is portrayed as *Head of all things*. The stone which was thrown on the scrap heap has become the 'capstone', the 'head of the corner', the 'corner-stone' (Matthew 21:42). Literally, the verse says, 'The stone which was rejected by the workmen has become the Head.' He is Head over all the created order of God. This has remarkable implications. From a human standpoint it means that all will ultimately recognize His headship. Let us not pervert this to produce universalism. It does not mean that all will be saved, but that all will be subjected to Christ either as Saviour or Judge. More powerful than this is the truth that even Satan will be subjected to Christ's power. His destiny is defeat; his fate is fire.

Christ is Head of all things. No wonder, then, that He is Head over the church. May God grant that we shall practically submit to that headship in all the activities and relationships within the church of Jesus Christ.

28.
It's right to obey

'Children **obey** *your parents'* (Eph. 6:1)
'Obey *your earthly masters'* (Eph. 6:5)

'Pray silence', called the master of ceremonies, 'for the Reverend Wayne Detzler.' It was a wedding reception, and I was asked to give thanks. The din of happy conversation came to a stop when the hotel employee in a smart dinner jacket shouted (incidentally in an Italian accent), 'Pray silence.' My mind raced to the evening service, when chatty church attenders often distracted me, and I wished I could employ the delightful Italian chap to introduce my sermons with the call: 'Pray silence.'

A nautical variant is the well-known cry heard on American ships: 'Now hear this.' Announcements designed to reach the ship's company are prefaced with this command. Every rating is expected to stop and listen and obey the order given over the speaker.

It is this sort of obedient hearing which is revealed in the Greek word translated in Ephesians 6 with 'obey'. The word *hupakouo* has as its root the word *akouo*, and this is seen in the English word 'acoustics'. The science of 'acoustics' helps people to hear, and the building with 'good acoustics' is one in which music or speech can easily be heard.

In the New Testament context, one who hears is expected to obey. 'He who has ears to hear', said the Lord repeatedly, 'let him hear.' Anyone who hears God's message is expected to obey it.

In Ephesians 6 the emphasis is on 'obedience'. Children are expected to 'hear and obey' their parents (Ephesians 6:1). This simple statement is loaded with meaning for the Christian church. In his marvellous little commentary, *Be Rich*,

Warren Wiersbe suggests four implications of this statement. First, the children are Christians and obeying their parents is an expression of Christian commitment. They are to be obedient 'in the Lord' (Ephesians 6:1). In fact, another translator phrased the command to emphasize this: 'Children obey in the Lord your parents.' The emphasis is not on parents being 'in the Lord' but on children obeying as an expression of their commitment.

A second aspect of childhood obedience is its rightness. Children are called to obey, because this is right (Ephesians 6:1). Just as the marriage relationship was part of created order and antedated the Mosaic law, so the children's obedience is right.

The divine command at Sinai gives obedience a place in biblical revelation. The third reason for obedience is God's express command. In fact, this commandment is the first with a specific promise. A general promise of blessing is linked to the second command in the Ten Commandments, but this one is the first to carry with it a special promise — long and peaceful life. In Exodus 20:12 and Deuteronomy 5:16 this promise is given.

Therefore, the fourth reason for obeying parents is the blessing which is attached to it. When young people rebel against their parents, they often incur pain. A habit may be developed which will be difficult to break in later life. A marriage may be contracted which will hamstring spiritual development for years to come. Attitudes towards spiritual things are formed which can only be displaced by years of spiritual application. This says nothing of the physical damage incurred by the abuse of drugs, alcohol or illicit sex. A Christian child who lives in obedience usually escapes these punishments inherent in rebellion.

Not only children are commanded to be obedient but so are 'slaves'. Subsequent exposition reveals that this principle of obedience at work applies to 'slave and free' men (Ephesians 6:8). Thus it has direct application to modern industry. Here, too, there are several applications to be mentioned.

First, this verse teaches that there is no distinction between the 'sacred and secular' in God's economy of things. No part of a Christian's life can be isolated from the other parts. When a Christian is at work in the office, shop or factory, he is serving the Lord just as really as when he is at worship. It was Latimer who said, 'Our Saviour Christ was a carpenter ... let no man disdain to follow Him in a common calling or occupation.' No occupation is common to the Christian; all are sacred.

Second, the Christian works to God's standards. Everything he does is done because we are 'slaves of Christ' (Ephesians 6:6). When a Christian shop assistant serves a customer, she does it as though that customer were the Lord. When a worker on the production line fits his small part to an aircraft motor, he knows that Christ is the ultimate Inspector of his work. The mother at home prepares each meal as though Christ were going to eat with the family.

Third, it is the Lord who rewards our work (Ephesians 6:8). The boss may be unappreciative of our work, and the trade union may press us to lower our standards. Christians know that the only approval which counts is from the Lord. When I was engaged in research at the university I came to realize that my supervisory professor was only an agent of the real Supervisor, and this enforced a much higher standard.

Obedience is not a matter of grudging adherence to the letter of the law. Biblical obedience is whole-hearted compliance which compels us to creative effort in serving the Lord. As spices add interest to the most mundane of foods, so working for God's glory makes our daily tasks meaningful.

Obey your signal

Some time ago I stopped at a complicated road intersection. There were several lights in various stages of red, green and amber. Next to these traffic lights was a very helpful sign: 'Obey your signal.'

Amid the confusion of life Christians see this sign: 'Obey your signal.' They look to the Word of God for signals which steer them safely through the maze of life's traffic. Our little word 'obey' is used in several ways to enlighten us and help us.

First, the most straightforward use of the Greek word is *simple obedience*. In Colossians 3 Paul repeated these commands. 'Children, obey your parents' (Colossians 3:20). 'Slaves, obey your earthly masters' (Colossians 3:22). This obedience is yet another aspect of submission, which is shown by Paul to be a fruit of the Spirit (Ephesians 5:21). In other words, Christians controlled by the Spirit will be marked by obedience to properly constituted authority in the home and at work. Rebellion against human authority is a sure sign of rebellion against the Spirit's control.

Second, the word is also used to indicate *obedience to sovereignty*. In Matthew 8:27 we read the astounded remark of Jesus' contemporaries when they saw that 'even the winds and the waves obey him'. Not only do natural forces bow to His command, but also the demons are forced to retreat by the word of the Lord (Mark 1:27). The sovereignty of God produces in nature and in the world of demons instant obedience. Obedience and sovereignty appear to be two sides of the same coin.

A third use of the word 'obey' relates to *salvation*. After Pentecost the church gained spiritual influence at Jerusalem, and 'a large number of priests became obedient to the faith' (Acts 6:7). Through the apostle Paul Gentiles were led to 'obey God' (Romans 15:18). What a magnificent definition of salvation this word gives us. Being saved is living in obedience to the gospel of God's grace. It is not the slavish subjection to a plethora of rules, as the Mormons, Seventh-Day Adventists, and British Israelites would insist. No, it is the Spirit-kindled obedience to the gospel by whch the Lord liberates us from sin's domination. Like the liberated slave in the Old Testament we go to the door and accept gladly the mark of obedient discipleship. (See Deuteronomy 15:17.)

There is a fourth use of the word translated 'obey'. It is seen in the story of Peter's release from prison. When he came to the house of Mary 'a servant girl named Rhoda came to answer the door' (Acts 12:13). The word translated 'answer' the door is our word 'obey'. Christians are those who always answer the door when God calls. When He seeks entrance into a given area of their lives, they are always ready to throw open the door. Only spiritual perverts like the Laodicean Christians in Revelation 3 bolt the door. Still the Lord stands at the door and knocks (Revelation 3:20). Be sure to 'obey', 'answer' the door when He speaks.

29.
Satan's schemes

'Take your stand against the devil's **schemes***'* (Eph. 6:11)

Martyn Lloyd-Jones reckoned that the greatest delusion perpetrated by the devil is the belief that he no longer exists. Aldous Huxley was no believer in God, but he said this of the devil: 'Few people now believe in the devil; but very many enjoy behaving as their ancestors behaved when the Fiend was a reality as unquestionable as his Opposite Number.'

Satan is sly by definition and he devotes all his attentions to creating chaos. The Bible calls him 'angel of light' (2 Corinthians 11:14), 'god of this age' (2 Corinthians 4:4), 'ruler of the kingdom of the air' (Ephesians 2:2) and 'the prince of this world' (John 14:30). He is also compared with some very dangerous inhabitants of the animal kingdom: 'serpent' (Genesis 3:4), and 'lion' (1 Peter 5:8).

In Ephesians 6:11 Paul describes Satan as a schemer. Christians are warned to combat the 'devil's schemes'. The word used here for 'schemes' is *methodeia*. Satan is a master of methods to trip up unsuspecting saints. In English the word 'method' is relatively neutral, but the Greeks imputed to it a uniformly negative meaning. Used relatively infrequently even in Greek literature, the word was often linked with the devil. It appears only in one other Bible verse, Ephesians 4:14. There Paul charges the Ephesians to grow up and avoid 'the cunning and craftiness of men in their deceitful scheming'.

It is not the schemes which I wish to emphasize, but the schemer, Satan himself. From Wartburg Martin Luther lamented, 'I can tell you in this idle solitude there are a thousand battles with Satan.'[1] John Calvin concurred with Luther on this point (if not on many others): 'Being forewarned of the constant presence of an enemy the most daring, the most powerful, the most crafty ... let us not allow ourselves to be overtaken by sloth or cowardice, but ... let us study to persevere.'[2] Samuel Rutherford, the Puritan preacher, put it this way: 'The devil's war is better than the devil's peace. Suspect dumb holiness. When the dog is kept out of doors he howls to be let in again.'[3]

Look out for Satan!

Shakespeare said, 'The devil hath power to assume a pleasing shape.' The Puritans often quoted Calvin in calling Satan the 'ape of God'. Paul warned the Corinthians that Satan could transform himself into an 'angel of light' (2 Corinthians 11:14). His stock in trade is deception, and his favourite targets are the Christians. In fact, the biblical names given to Satan all relate to his role as the pest of the pious.

First, he is called the *devil*, which means the accuser. In Revelation 12:10-11 the Spirit-inspired apostle John explained how this can be applied. The devil is like a carp. Carp, together with other fish, are scavengers. They sweep the bottom of the pond looking for all sorts of unappetizing titbits. (At least, they would not appeal to the human palate!) The devil dredges up the unsavoury past of every Christian in order to plague him with it. He is like a blackmailer who constantly reminds Christians of some sin. His hope is to lure them into the same sin or some similarly damaging one. A Christian can forget Bible verses with ease. He can also blot out of his mind hymns, and sleep quite easily excludes sermons. There is absolutely no problem involved in forgetting spiritual truth. To forget sin committed in the past, however, requires supernatural ability. The devil does his best to keep those memories alive.

An off-colour joke heard years ago can be recalled completely, including the 'punch line'. A sexual experience before marriage can be relived at will. Lies told in the past are like leeches fixing themselves to one's memory. The devil accuses us of these over and over again, neglecting the biblical truth that our sins are buried in the deepest sea.

In Revelation we have the answer to this devilish accusation. Christians are to overcome the devil 'with the blood of the Lamb and the word of our testimony' (Revelation 12:11). It is the sacrifice of the Saviour which provides a complete cure for our sinfulness. Our past testimony of forgiveness reminds us of the faithfulness and competence of God to deal with all the dirt of our pre-conversion life.

A second name applied to the Evil One is *Satan*. Satan means the 'adversary'. The apostle Peter warned contemporary Christians that Satan prowled about like a lip-licking lion trying to gobble up unsuspecting saints (1 Peter 5:8). The great adversary of spiritual growth is none other than Satan.

A recent issue of one Christian magazine portrayed a pyjama-clad, yawning saint comfortably situated in bed. The caption told all: 'The Quiet Time — A Big Yawn?' It is Satan himself who convinces Christians that extra sleep will sort out spiritual problems. Joseph Hall, the Puritan-sympathizing Bishop of Norwich, wrote, 'Satan rocks the cradle when we sleep at our devotions.'

When we go to worship distractions abound. A bawling baby or a barking dog can put both the preacher and the listener off his stroke. I remember one time preaching in a midwestern American village. To my shock a bat made lazy circles around the makeshift church. Once the bat was slain, three dogs wandered in through the open door. One can easily concentrate on television or the newspaper, but try to focus on the preaching of the Word, and Satan creates a rainbow array of diversions.

Satan grudgingly admitted the presence of Christ in the world. He saw twelve men commit themselves to discipleship in response to the Lord's call. But when Jesus spoke of crucifixion Satan moved Peter to protest. So vehement and so satanic was that protest, that Jesus rebuked him with the words: 'Out of my sight, Satan!' (Matthew 16:23.) Satan to this very day is causing Christians to resist spiritual truth. In the most biblical of churches one discovers sincere Christians with strangely perverted beliefs. Satan is the adversary of spiritual truth. Peter told the Christians to 'resist him, standing firm in the faith' (1 Peter 5:9).

One final name is applied frequently to our enemy. He is the *'tempter'* par excellence. It was this aspect of the devil's devices which appeared most prominently in the Lord's earthly life. In Matthew 4 we find the tempter trying to lead astray the Lord. To us this appears ridiculous, but the Lord took Satan seriously and answered him firmly. Does not this teach us never to trifle with the Evil One?

It was David, the great warrior king, who exemplified this weapon in the adversary's armour. Butchering a lion and a bear was possible. Slaying a blasphemous giant was accomplished. Establishing a kingdom with an army of misfits was done. But resisting the attraction of a woman seemed beyond his ability. Satan brought him down like a mighty oak with a rotten heart.

Satan uses a plethora of projectiles to pierce the Christian's defences. Evil thoughts arise in one's mind before the day begins, and one has the impression that Satan has been hatching them during the night. Satan also introduces into our consciousness a dart of fear. Future illness, disaster or death sometimes assume proportions of obsession, and Satan thus paralyses Christians. Overconfidence is yet another tool of the tempter. He urges Christians to rest on past performance. After an uplifting Christian conference come the temptations of everyday life. Following a great spiritual victory one often stumbles over some spiritual pebble in the path. One of my fellow elders usually warns baptismal candidates to be on their guard against inevitable temptation. Most stand firm, but some have fallen flat on their spiritual faces. Jesus warned us that temptation can only be countered with the Word of God. 'It is written' was the main weapon in the Lord's arsenal, and it should also be ours.

Christians are declared by the Word to be 'more than conquerors' (Romans 8:37). Spiritual victory over Satan requires steadfast resistance and this is based on three pillars. First, one must have a storehouse of memorized Scripture with which to face the foe. Second, the name of Jesus must be used in prayer as a rebuke against the Great Pretender. Third, every Christian needs a spiritual brother or sister with whom he or she can pray in a time of temptation. Remember that 'having disarmed the powers and authorities, he made a public spectacle of them, triumphing over them by the cross' (Colossians 2:15).

[1] R. Bainton, *Here I Stand*, p.194
[2] J. Calvin, *Institutes*, I, p.151

30.
Christian armour

*'Put on the full **armour** of God'* (Eph. 6:13)

In our day armour is coming back into style. When demonstrations or riots threaten, the police appear in a modern version of armour. Their helmets are an easily recognized symbol of British law and order. To this standard protective equipment is now added a bullet-proof vest. It protects the vital organs, just as the breastplate guarded soldiers of the ancient world. Finally, a riot shield is issued when serious danger threatens. These are heavy plastic rectangles designed to fend off thrown missiles, such as rocks, bricks and bottles. Today's armour may be more functional than beautiful, but it fulfils the same role as its Roman predecessor.

Paul urges Christians to be protected with a spiritual armour. The word he uses is *panoplia*, and it is transliterated into our English word 'panoply'. To us it means a complete covering, a full armour.

Paul lived in close contact with Roman soldiers. This was not his choice, but God's. Such close contact resulted in the conversion of men in the imperial guard (Philippians 1:13; 4:22). In fact, the New Testament paints Roman soldiers in a positive light. The centurion at the cross recognized Christ's deity. Christ healed the centurion's child. Cornelius was a spiritually sensitive centurion, whose whole household was converted through his influence. While Paul was being taken under guard to Rome, it was the centurions who intervened to save the apostle's life (Acts 23:23; 27:43). These positive statements must, of course, be offset against the callous soldiers who gambled for the Lord's garments while His life poured out of His slashed side and pierced hands and feet (John 19:24).

In the first century Roman soldiers were a common sight throughout the empire. Everyone knew about their armour, and feared their weapons. Under the Spirit's inspiration Paul turned this to spiritual capital. He urged Christians to 'put on the armour of light' (Romans 13:12). The weapons of righteousness were to be taken in both hands (2 Corinthians 6:7). Again in 2 Corinthians 10:4 he warned that our weapons are not from the arsenal of the world, rather they are charged with 'divine power to demolish strongholds'.

Paul emphasizes the conflict with Satan and the world. He is desperately concerned that Christians be armed and protected for this battle. The armour he describes was not designed for the parade ground but for the battlefield. Throughout Ephesians 6 runs the persistent truth that we are in constant conflict and must be on our guard.

No Achilles' heel

Achilles was Homer's archetypal hero. Like a Wild West star he triumphed over all enemies. His style was grand and his appearance melted hearts. Achilles was invincible until an arrow from Paris pierced his unprotected heel. This classic case of negligence is illustrated in the spiritual life of thousands of Christians. Their strength is formidable, until Satan strikes at their weak point and they tumble down. Paul presents in Ephesians 6:13-17 a complete armour designed to cover the Christians with spiritual protection.

The *belt of truth* (v.14) served a dual purpose. It held the armour together and it supported the sword. Truth is the essential spiritual element, and it refers here to genuineness and sincerity. The Christian must be clothed with a sincere desire to live for the Lord. He speaks truthfully and lovingly (Ephesians 4:15) and thus he combats deceitfulness (Ephesians 5:6-9). God desires truth in the inner man (Psalm 51:6). This guards against the two aspects of hypocrisy: self-righteousness and worldliness. *Question*: Are you sincere about spiritual warfare?

The *breastplate of righteousness* (v.14) protected the vital organs from well-aimed arrows. There was apparently no covering for the back, and this helped to guard against unauthorized retreat. Righteousness is a loaded word in the New Testament. It is God's answer to our past sin (Romans 1:17) and it is also God's enabling for the Christian life (1 Corinthians 1:30). Many modern cults tell us that we are saved by keeping the law of God, for example, Mormonism, Jehovah's Witnesses, British Israelitism, etc. The Bible tells us that righteousness is deposited to our account by God's grace. Righteousness also refers to the quality of our life. 'How do you react when your garden is vandalized?' a friend asked me. This pointed up the truth that righteousness has more to do with our reactions than it does with our planned actions. *Question*: Are you living the kind of life which enables you to do spiritual battle?

Feet shod with the gospel of peace are always 'on the go' for God (v.15). Julius Caesar's troops were successful in battle for many reasons. One of these was their strong footwear which enabled them to cover great distances and surprise their enemies. The gospel equips us with peace. We are at peace with God and man (Ephesians 2:15-17). We can thus devote ourselves to spiritual battle because our hearts are at peace. It is stress that kills, not hard work. This gospel of peace keeps us going, witnessing incessantly for the Lord and endeavouring to point sinners to the Saviour. Paul found the feet of a witness to be beautiful when they marched through the land shod with gospel peace (Romans 10:15; cf. Isaiah 57:2). *Questions*: Are you prepared to fight spiritual battles? Have you got your boots on, or are you lolling in the back pew with your slippers on?

The *shield of faith* (v.16) gives us something to hide behind when the satanic arrows are flying. The shield mentioned here was very large, four feet by two and a half feet. It was a door of protection against the enemies' arrows, many of which had been dipped in an inflammable substance and lit. When the battle raged shields could be linked to form a wall of defence. The Old Testament refers to God as our shield

(Proverbs 30:5). The New Testament insists that our faith is the ultimate in protection against satanic onslaughts (1 John 5:4). When the piercing arrows of depression, anger and fear are filling the air, we take refuge behind the shield of faith. Together as believers we link our faith-shields to ward off the devil's darts. *Question*: Are you able to defend yourself against Satan's attack?

The *helmet of salvation* (v.17) protects the brain from flying objects. Romans wore helmets fashioned out of leather and brass. Only a well-aimed blow from an axe or a hammer could crack them. Thus the Christian is protected by salvation from the axe of doubt which would split his spiritual life. When doubts arise concerning our salvation, we are reminded that the Lord will finish what He has started (Philippians 1:6). When doubts concerning the Word of God are aimed at us, we shield our minds with the salvation which gives us an understanding hidden to unregenerate man. No wonder he doubts. His mind is clouded over by Satan's fog. When doubts arise about other Christians in our fellowship, we recall that they too are objects of God's eternal rescue operation. *Question*: Is your mind guarded by God's salvation?

Finally, we have the single offensive weapon in the armour, the *sword of the Spirit* (v.17). Paul here referred to the short sword designed for close combat. This is the Word of God, the Bible. The Holy Spirit is the Source and Author of the Bible (2 Peter 1:21). Because the Word of God is inspired it penetrates to the darkest recesses of human thought and emotion (Hebrews 4:12). When temptation assails the saint, he follows Christ's example and wields the sword of the Word (Matthew 4:4). When opportunity arises to share an evangelistic word, the sword of the Spirit pricks consciences and opens them to the saving work of God. It was Dwight L. Moody, the nineteenth-century American preacher, who regarded with horror the onset of liberal theology. 'A mutilated Bible', Moody warned in his rustic accents, 'is a broken sword.' The whole of divine revelation must be brought to bear on Christian life and witness. *Question*: Have you learned the art of offensive warfare?

The Christian armour was needed in the Roman world, but it is even more necessary in these days of apocalyptic expectation. Satan stands in full array against the saints singularly and collectively. For this reason Paul warned the Romans: 'Our salvation is nearer now than when we first believed. The night is nearly over; the day is almost here. So let us put aside the deeds of darkness and put on the armour of light' (Romans 13:11-12).

31.
Prayer in the Spirit

'And **pray** in the Spirit'   (Eph. 6:18)
'**Pray** also for me'   (Eph. 6:19)
'**Pray** that I may declare it fearlessly'   (Eph. 6:20)

If the Bible is the Christian's diet, prayer is his breathing. Both are absolutely essential to Christian living. Paul states this priority quite clearly by using the Greek word *proseuchomai*. Its root meaning is 'directed approach'; one prays specifically *to* the Lord. The word for 'prayer' (*euchomai*) is rendered more intense by the preposition 'towards' (*pros*).

From the first, Christians have appreciated the indispensability of prayer. Christian writers have expended their best efforts in eulogizing it. Thomas Chalmers, the great Scottish preacher, said, 'Prayer does not enable us to do a greater work for God. Prayer is a greater work for God.'

D.L. Moody, the Chicago evangelist, saw prayer as being essential. 'The Christian on his knees', he claimed, 'sees more than the philosopher on tiptoe.' Moody was not an educated man, but he was endowed with remarkable spiritual discernment.

Leonard Ravenhill, the revival writer, placed prayer high on the list of spiritual disciplines. 'The self-sufficient do not pray, the self-satisfied will not pray, the self-righteous cannot pray,' Ravenhill rightly judged. 'No man is greater than his prayer life.'

Perhaps the most pithy little comment on prayer was scrawled on a London wall during the blitz: 'If your knees are knocking,' the anonymous sage scribbled, 'kneel on them.'

Paul fuelled this sort of statement in his conclusion to the Ephesian letter. First he asserted that 'everyone needs prayer' (Ephesians 6:18). He inserted four 'alls'. Therefore the Christian prays 'on *all* occasions'. Prayer is as appropriate beside the cot of a newborn baby as it is beside the bed of a dying saint. Prayer can be mingled with the laughter of joy and the salty tears of despair. Paul also urged '*all* kinds of prayers'. Praise dare not be omitted, but neither should petition be absent from our prayer. God delights in hearing and answering our requests. One must pray 'always', at *all* times. In another place Paul put it this way: 'Pray without ceasing.' Just as a loved one is never absent from the lover's thoughts, so the Lord must never be absent from the Christian's mind. Prayer is a life-style. Finally Paul urges that prayers be made for '*all* the saints'. How sad are those mistakenly self-sufficient Christians who try to muddle through without the prayer support of their spiritual brothers and sisters!

Paul sets the example by repetition in Ephesians 6:19: 'Pray also for me.' He was under house arrest in Rome (Acts 28:30-31). His former freedom was now severely restricted. He could no longer visit those fellow believers whose spiritual welfare weighed so heavily upon his heart. Since he could not go to them, God brought them to him (Acts 28:31). The prayers of the Ephesians were answered in that way.

Paul requested prayer that he might be fearless in his witness for the Lord. Somehow I never think of Paul as being timid, but he felt the need for extra courage to meet extraordinary suffering (Ephesians 6:20). That this occurred, is also seen in Acts 28. The final verse of Acts states it this way: 'Boldly and without hindrance he preached the kingdom of God and taught about the Lord Jesus Christ' (Acts 28:31).

Prayer power prevails

My father-in-law was pastor of the church where we worshipped during my teenage years. He would often invite people to attend the midweek prayer meeting and Bible study. Then he would add, 'The prayer meeting is the powerhouse of the church.' His ministry in a suburb of industrial Detroit proved the validity of this assessment. Prayer is powerful when it comes from a righteous person's mouth (James 5:16). There are three main focuses of prayer.

First, prayer is powerful in one's own life. We pray for *ourselves*. We have all seen the motto: 'Prayer changes things.' It could be amended to read, 'Prayer changes me.' As John Owen, the Puritan preacher wrote, 'He who prays as he ought will endeavour to live as he prays.'

Solomon's prayer was for wisdom. He implored God to give him the understanding and discernment necessary to govern God's people (1 Kings 3:9). God answered and added to wisdom wealth and power.

Hezekiah the king of Judah was informed by Isaiah the prophet that his life was drawing to an end. 'Put your affairs in order, because God is going to take you,' the prophet said. Hezekiah implored God to extend his life, and the Lord did so (Isaiah 38). As proof of this coming blessing, God turned back the shadow on the sundial.

Perhaps the most urgent personal prayer occurred at the crucifixion. One of the thieves slain beside the Saviour was unrepentant until the end. He had scorned God in life and did so in death. The other, however, saw the divine wisdom of Calvary, and he begged the Lord: 'Remember me when you come into your kingdom.' The instant response of the suffering Saviour was this: 'Today you will be with me in paradise' (Luke 23:43). God answers prayer when we pray for ourselves in accordance with His will.

A second focus of prayer is our *fellow man*. E.M. Bounds, who wrote the little classic *Power Through Prayer*, summed up this intercessory responsibility: 'Talking to men for God is a great thing, but talking to God for men is greater still.' William Law said it even more succinctly: 'There is nothing that makes us love a man so much as praying for him.'

Abraham was a great man of God and his obedience is exemplary. He was the prototype of saints justified by faith. Abraham was also a great intercessor. This was demonstrated when he prayed for his wayward nephew Lot, and God saved Lot out of the sin-sick city of Sodom (Genesis 18-19).

Moses was another example of power through prayer. He despatched Joshua to lead the Israelites into battle against the

Amalekites. While Joshua did battle, Moses prayed on the hilltop. The old leader stood with hands raised (and even propped up) praying as long as the battle lasted. The result was victory for Israel through prayer (Exodus 17).

When Peter was jailed at Jerusalem the Christians gathered in the home of Mary to pray. While they interceded, God intervened. The jail was miraculously opened and Peter was led out. So astounded were the Christians that they almost failed to open the door and receive the delivered apostle (Acts 12).

The final focus of prayer is the most important, for it is the *glory of God*. The main beneficiary of prayer is neither ourselves nor others; it is the glory of our great God. Charles Kingsley had it right when he wrote, 'The very act of prayer honours God and gives glory to God, for it confesses that God is what He is.'

When Elijah confronted the prophets of Baal on Mt Carmel, the prophet was not concerned with his reputation. Under wicked old Ahab prophets enjoyed neither long life nor general public respect. Elijah was also not concerned to prove his ability to perform miracles. His primary purpose was to reassert the glory of Jehovah. In answer to his prayer Jehovah revealed His power, humiliated the Baal establishment, and won the hearts of His fickle people (1 Kings 18).

Stephen was in a similar situation. He was on trial for his life. Christianity had become to the Jewish leaders a very painful thorn in the flesh. When they pressed Stephen he prayed that God's glory would be revealed. The immediate result was a storm of stones which crushed the life out of that early Christian martyr. The ultimate result was the conversion of Saul of Tarsus, perhaps the greatest preacher of the early church (Acts 7:54-60). God had the glory.

Prayer is not only a high priority for Christians, it was a primary emphasis in the earthly life of our Lord. At a time of temptation He prayed. When weariness overtook Him, He prayed. On the Mount of Transfiguration He was praying. On the eve of His crucifixion He lingered in the garden of prayer. He taught His disciples to pray, and He prayed for you

and me before He died (John 17:20). Now He lives in glory
with the Father, where 'He always lives to intercede' for us
(Hebrews 7:25).

32.
The faithful servant

'The dear brother and faithful **servant***'* (Eph. 6:21)

In modern society service seems to be a dying virtue. Many will have endured the television programme, *Are You Being Served?* Based upon the antics of shop assistants in a departmental store, the episodes revolved more around intrigue and entertainment than around the service to customers. In a sad way this is symptomatic of our diseased days. Most are more interested in their own enjoyment than in serving others.

From the New Testament onwards, Christianity has stood out against the prevailing wind. The characteristic demeanour of a true disciple is service. 'The object of love is to serve,' concluded the scholar president Woodrow Wilson, 'not to win.' An anonymous writer summarized service most cogently: 'Service is the rent we pay for the space we occupy.'

Two words in the New Testament describe service. The more common term is *doulos* (slave). Reference here is made to the bondslaves who comprised a large proportion of Roman society. They were owned completely and exploited rather ruthlessly by their masters. Paul often used this term to describe himself as a 'bondslave' of the Lord Jesus Christ. Christ's possession of Paul was complete, and there was no hint of exploitation. Tychicus, Paul's faithful companion, was called in Colossians 4:7, a 'fellow slave'.

Tychicus was also called a 'faithful servant' in Ephesians 6:21 and Colossians 4:7. The word employed here is not *doulos* (bondslave) but *diakonos* (servant). Obviously *diakonos* is closely connected to our word 'deacon'. Its roots are *dia* (through) and *konin* (dust). A servant or deacon is, therefore, one who 'goes through the dust' for another. However, these roots were rather lost even in the apostolic age.

Paul claimed in Ephesians 3:7 that he was a 'servant (*diakonos*) of the gospel'. His whole efforts were devoted to serving the cause of gospel proclamation. Whether he was in prison under house arrest or dashing around the Mediterranean basin, Paul served the gospel. Obviously, 'service' carries with it an aura of hard work and submission.

Tychicus was seen to be '*a faithful servant* of the Lord' (Ephesians 6:21). 'Service' and faithfulness go hand in hand. No wonder that Paul heaped upon Tychicus such praise. In fact, in Colossians 4:7-14 there appear seven men who were marked by their allegiance to the prisoner Paul. Like the Lord, Paul surrounded himself with faithful men (2 Timothy 2:2). The old adage is true: 'The greatest ability is reliability.'

At your service

The word *diakonos* (deacon, servant) is used widely in the New Testament. It always denotes duty rather than office. What a person did in serving the Saviour was far more important than any title he bore. In fact, the early church was rather weak on the idea of office. 'Apostles' were quite literally 'sent ones'. 'Evangelists' spread the good news to those who had not yet heard. 'Pastor-teachers' were shepherds of the flock exercising pastoral care wedded to practical teaching. By the same token, 'deacon' was used in several contexts to describe service in general and Christian service in particular.

First, service related to the menial employee who *served tables*. When the Lord attended and enhanced the wedding at Cana in Galilee, the agents who carried out His commands were 'servants' who drew the water, carried the wine and generally did the master's bidding (John 2:5-9). In our day servants in private homes have been largely replaced by sophisticated machinery and temporary help. The 'service man' who comes to care for those machines is a highly-paid expert who is more in control of the situation than he is in service to the housewife beleaguered by broken-down appliances.

Second, the term 'service' is often translated with *minister*. Paul claimed he was a 'servant, through whom you came to believe' (1 Corinthians 3:5). Paul's inspired advice to young Timothy was designed to develop him as 'a good minister (servant) of Christ' (1 Timothy 4:6). The Christian minister must always be a servant, serving the other Christians and serving the world with the bread of life. This service must also be seen in his approach to the community. Some years ago my brother-in-law was pastor of a small congregation outside Chicago. On the church minibus he had painted the words: 'We are your servants for Jesus' sake' (2 Corinthians 4:5). This attitude of service was further underlined by correspondence with a very dear colleague. He usually closed each letter with the phrase: 'Yours in co-labourship'. His English grammar might have been challenged, but the spiritual attitude was exactly right.

Third, the office of service was given the name *deacon* (servant). It arose first in Acts 6:2 when the apostles judged it unwise to leave the 'ministry of the word ... to wait on (*diakonein*) tables'. That little phrase 'wait on tables' has given rise to two interpretations. It may have meant the serving of food. An alternative interpretation was working at the 'money tables' in the financial affairs of the church (Jamieson, Fausset and Brown). Although the word 'deacon' never appears in the English translation of Acts 6, it is obviously there in the original Greek as a verb 'to serve'. In Philippians 1:1 Paul addresses himself to the 'overseers [bishops] and deacons', and to Timothy Paul gave specific instruction concerning the deacons (1 Timothy 3:8 ff).

When the Bible speaks of 'deacons' or servants of the church, it emphasizes what they do rather than the office they possess. They are to be committed men first and committee men only secondarily. As I write, my mind is filled with thanksgiving for that deacon who arose in the middle of the night to locate and repair a leak in our church roof. There is another one who cheerfully took over the chief steward's work and thus immeasurably adds to our services. Men who have served as church secretary are dearer than brothers to me because of their faithful support. When I see the deacons sitting at the communion table, I think of the 'behind-the-scenes' work which they shoulder to make our ministry possible.

There is a fourth use of the word, and it relates to *women who serve*, to the 'deaconess'. The Bible record reveals God's concern for individuals and gives us the names of the women who 'helped to support' (served) the Lord Jesus Christ. There was Mary Magdalene, that trophy of grace who had been rescued from demonic control. Joanna was the wife of Herod's palace manager. Susanna was distinguished for her service (Luke 8:2-3).

At Cenchrea Phoebe was the 'servant of the church' (Romans 16:1). The word used to describe Phoebe was 'deaconess' (servant). Emphasis here lies not on her office but her service. She rendered invaluable service to the apostle and to the church.

Missions have been blessed with many such servants. One thinks of such distinguished sisters as Mary Slessor, Gladys Aylward, Amy Carmichael and Frances Ridley Havergal.

In fact, Christ taught His men that the dominant characteristic of Christians would be service. Men of worldly wisdom are concerned to 'get on' and build their career. Position is the carrot which lures them ever onward at an awful price. Christ taught His disciples: 'Not so with you. Instead, whoever wants to become great among you must be your servant, and whoever wants to be first must be your slave' (Matthew 20:26-27).

When one serves faithfully, one realizes that the rewards will be handed out by the Lord. In fact, the reward will be with the Lord in glory. 'Where I am, my servant also will be,' promises the Lord. 'My Father will honour the one who serves me' (John 12:26).